Bob Joseph and Bart E. Slyp have given birth to the funniest fetus you ever met. He's street-smart and wise beyond his period of gestation. His trash talking commentary is so outrageously provocative, you'll want to wash his mouth out with soap. But you can't you dumb sh*t because he hasn't been born yet!

Text and Pictures Copyright
©2021 Bob Joseph and Bart E. Slyp
All rights reserved under International and Pan-American Copyright Conventions.
No part of this publication may be reproduced, stored in retrieval system, or transmitted, in any form or by any means, electronic, mechanical, photocopying, recording, or otherwise without the prior permission of the Copyright owner.

This book may be purchased in bulk for promotional, educational, or business use.
Please contact bob@andbob.com
ISBN 978-1-7335422-3-4

Published by IngramSpark
for bobart books

THE MOTHER of ALL BOOKS
EMBRYO!

by

Bob Joseph & Bart E. Slyp

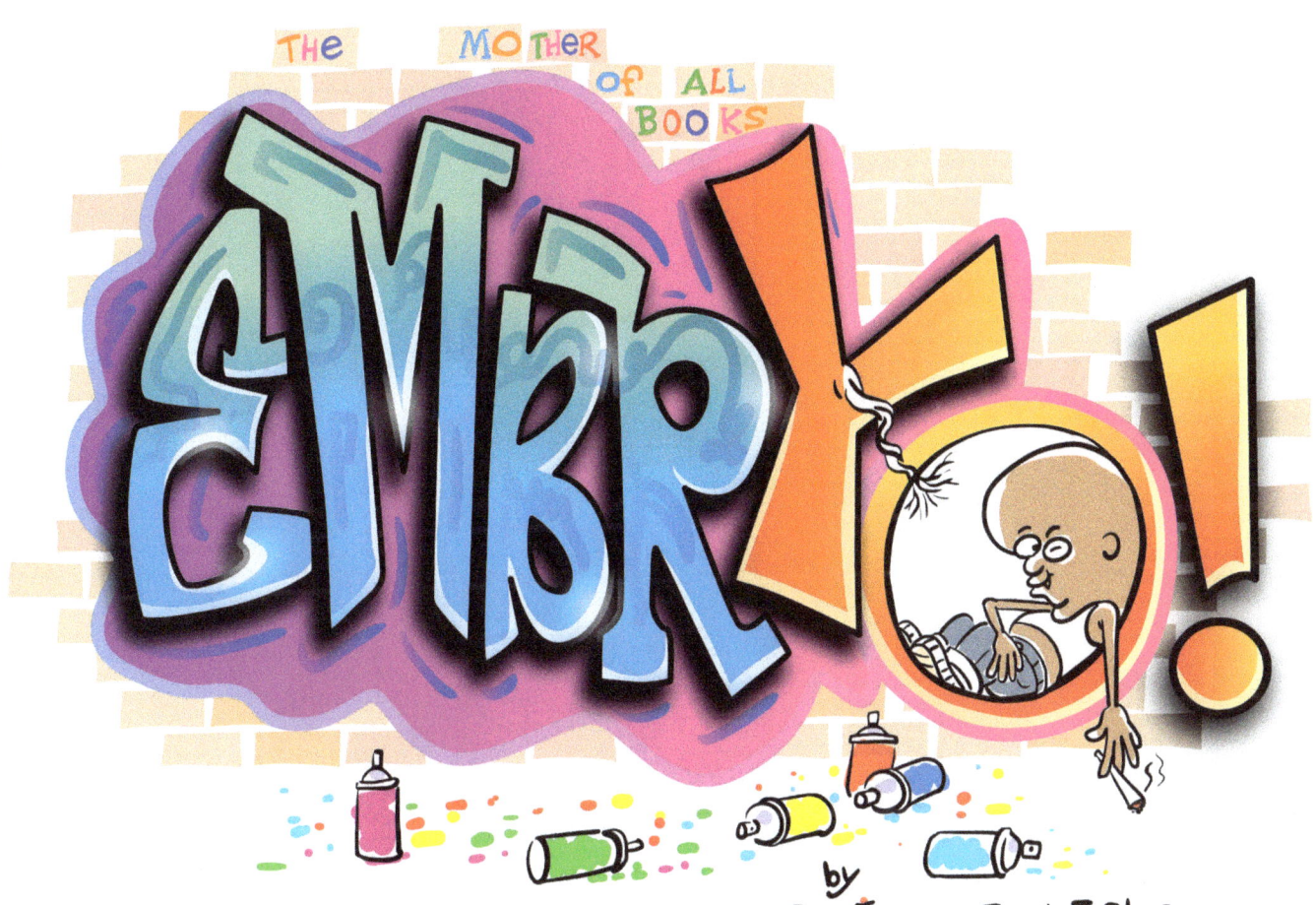

TRUST ME
WE CAN'T DO THAT!

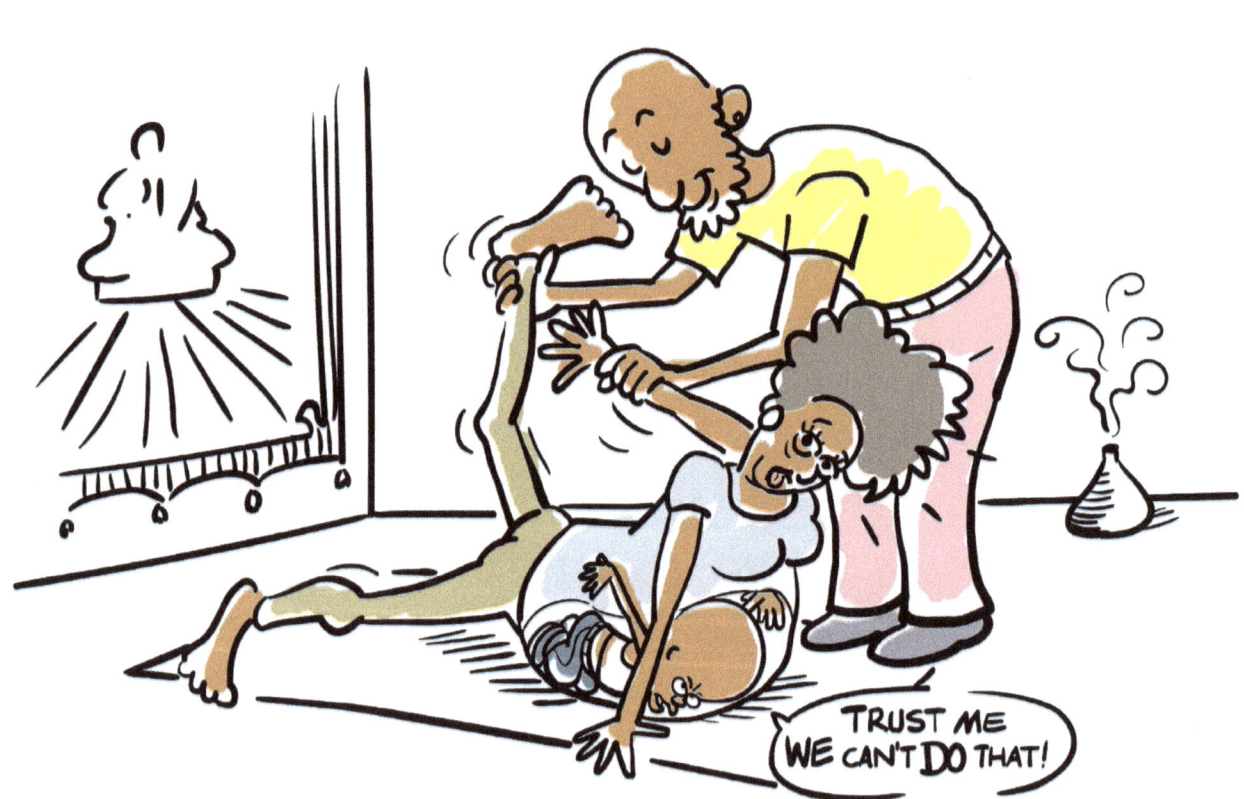

YOU CAN LET ME OFF RIGHT HERE... BEFORE THAT MOTHERF@!!!KIN' HILL!

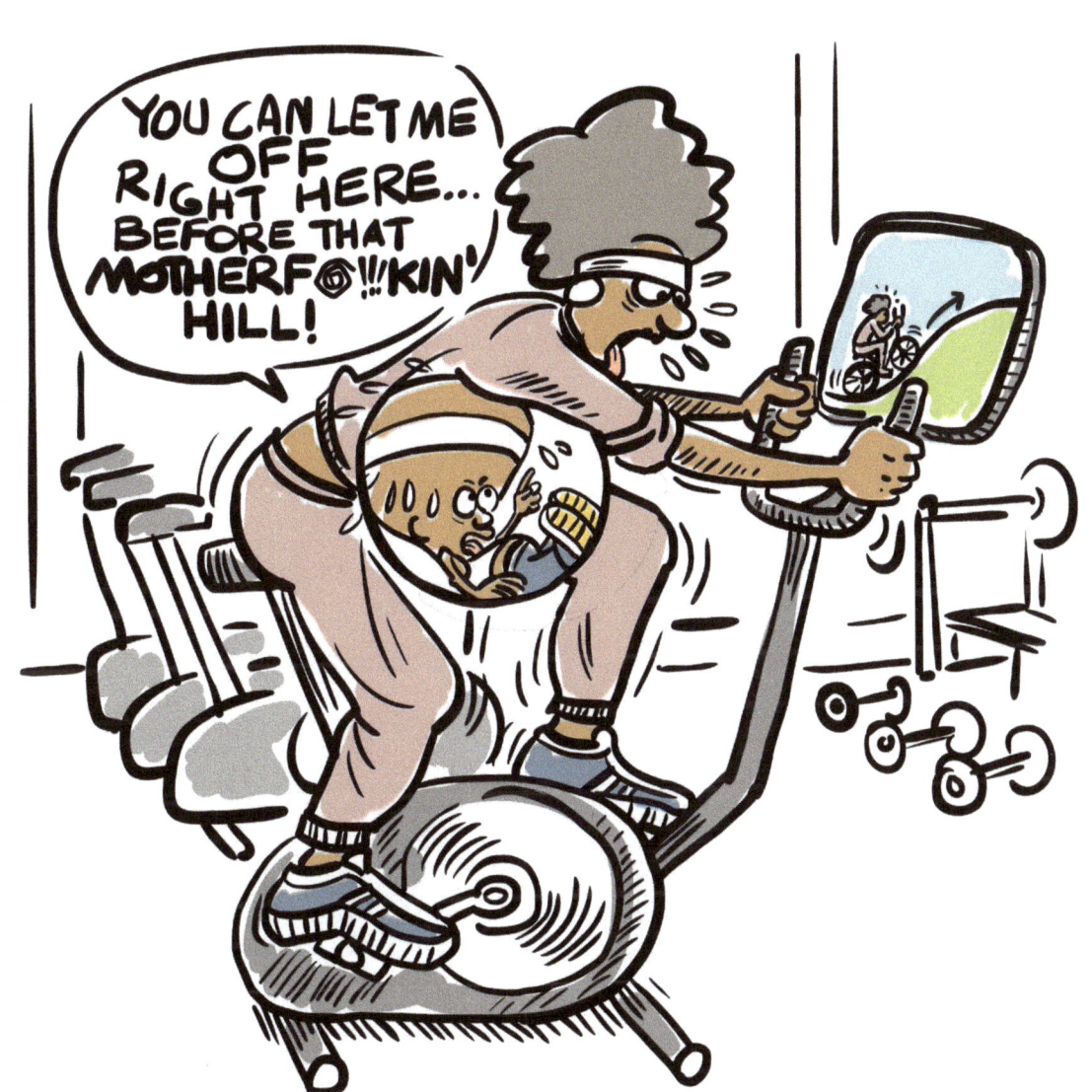

FROZEN FOOD
veggie
gies
PIZZA ROLLS
PIZZA ROLLS
HOT POCKETS
HOT POCKETS
HOT POCKETS
CHICKEN WINGS
CHICKEN WINGS
CHICKEN WINGS
CHICKEN WINGS
PUKE YELLOW CURRY
PUKE YELLOW CURRY
PUKE YELLOW CURRY
PUKE YELLOW CURRY
MAC 'N CHEESE BITES
MAC 'N CHEESE BITES
GMO TATER TOTS
GMO TATER TOTS
GMO TATER TOTS
TOASTER STRUDEL
BONELESS CHICKEN BITES
BEEF FRANKS IN A BLANKET
BEEF FRANKS IN A BLANKET
CHICKEN CARBONARA
CHICKEN CARBONARA
HAM BURGERS
HAM BURGERS
F K FRESH! FROZEN'S WHERE IT'S AT!!!

I REMEMBER WHEN I WAS YOUR AGE... I THOUGHT I WAS A F!!!@KING FISH!
PARENTS
OCTUPLETS

PFFFFFF
I AGREE WITH MOMMA... THE REAL ESTATE BUBBLE IS ABOUT TO BURST!

HAHAHA!
HAHAHA!
I GOT ONE! A WOMAN WALKS INTO A BAR ... AND 3 MONTHS LATER I MAGICALLY APPEAR!

YESSSSSS!!
BZZZZZZZZ
YESSSSSSSSS!!

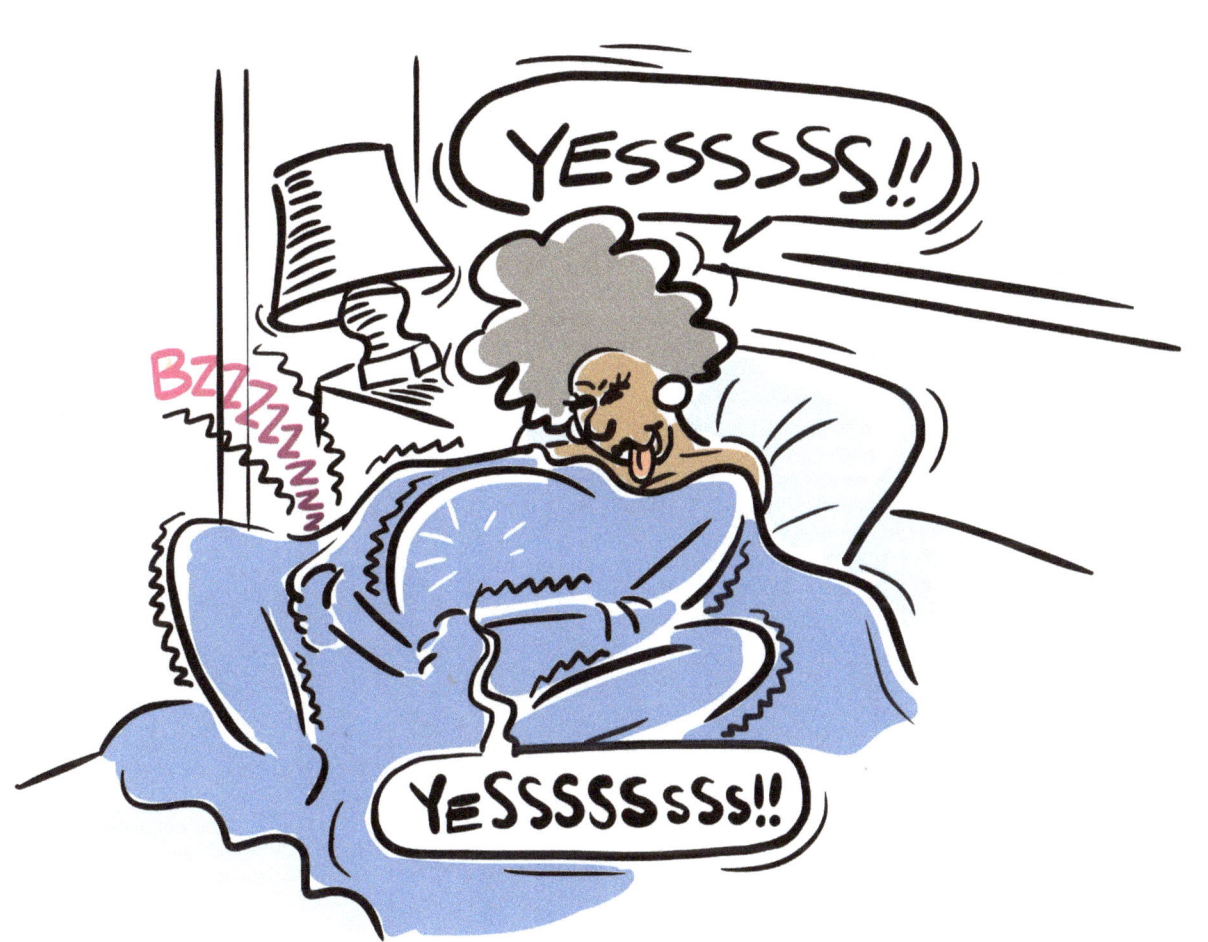

SO YOU'RE THE MOTHER F@!!!KER!

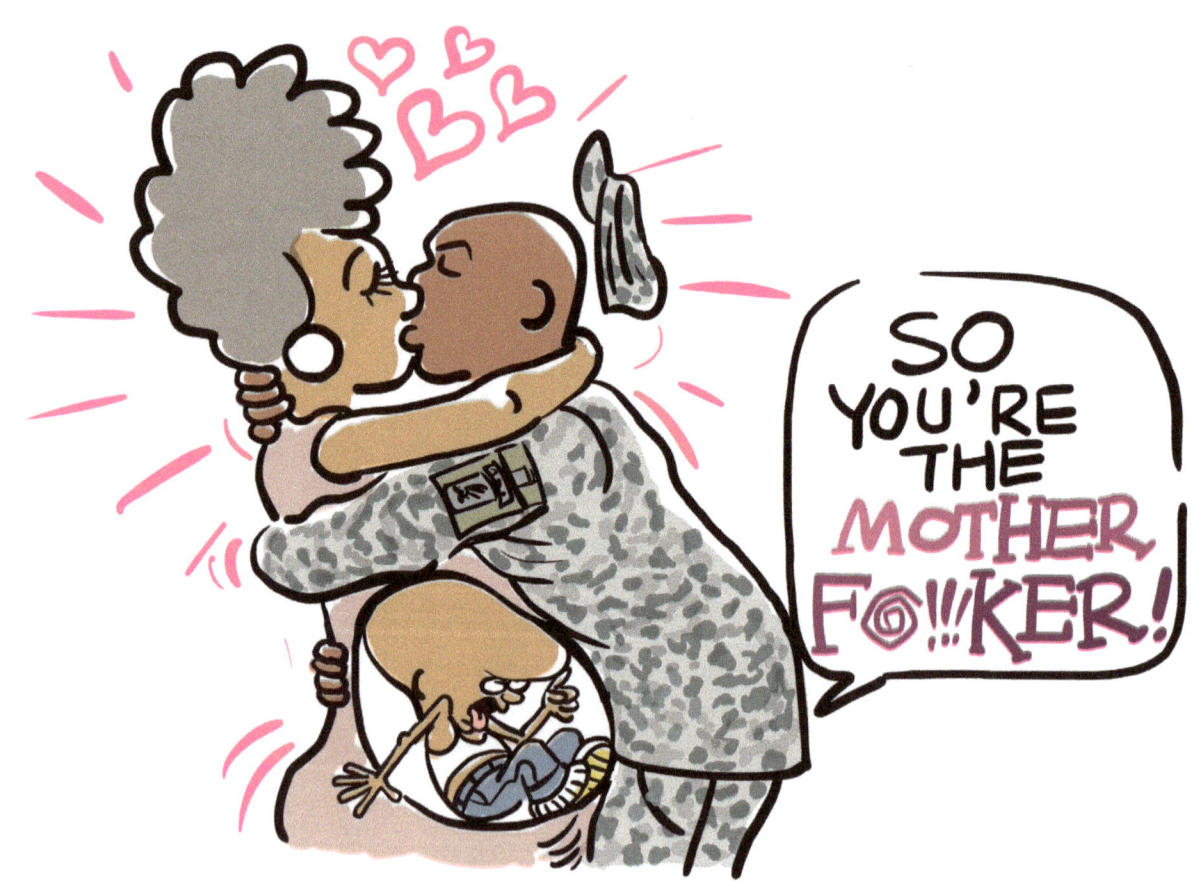

I DON'T CARE IF YOU'RE HER HUSBAND I'M GETTING THE FIRST DANCE!!!

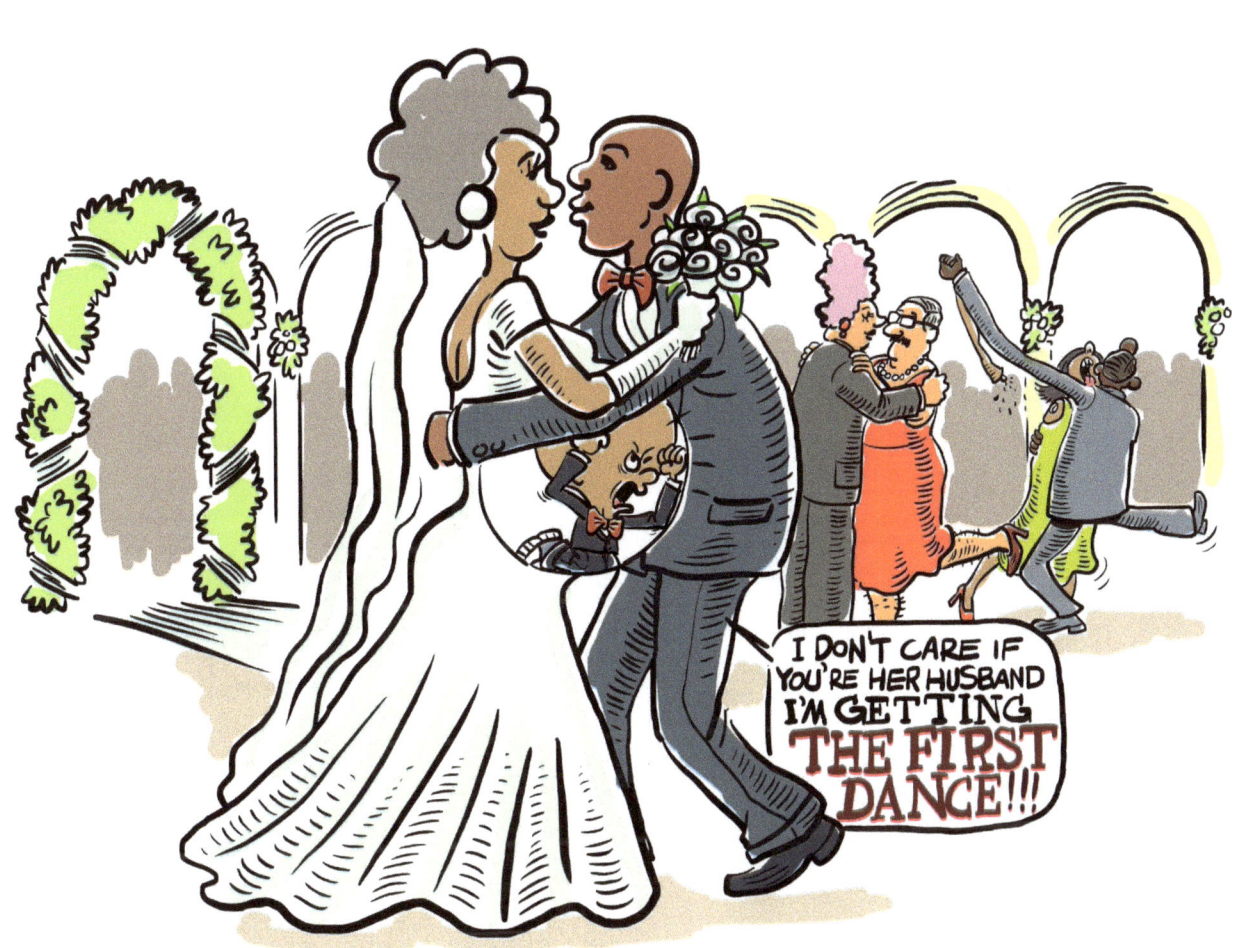

#%@
CHRIS R*CK SPECIAL
YOU F@!!!KIN' OK WITH ALL THAT F!!@KIN' CURSIN'?

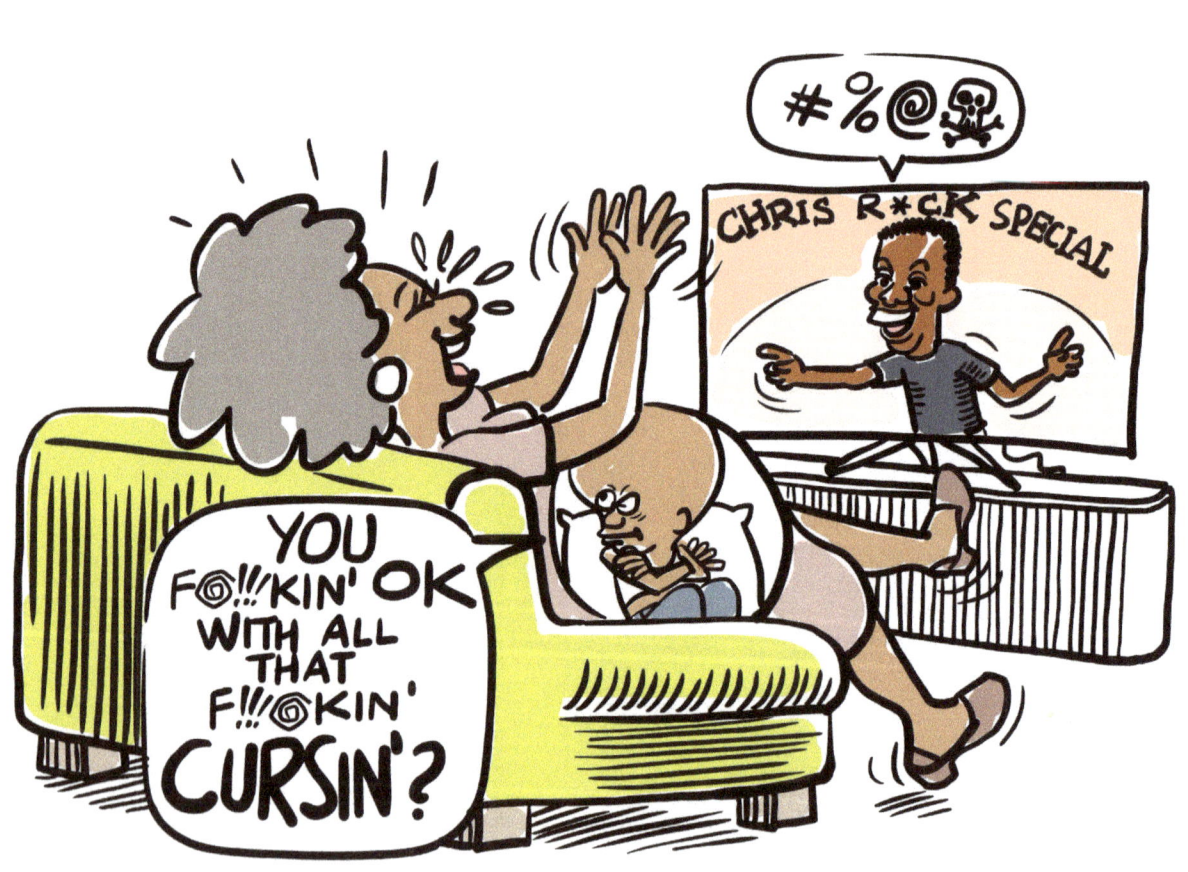

SQUEAK! SQUEAK! SQUEAK! SQUEAK!
OMG! HERE'S THAT F**KING SNAKE AGAIN!! THIS TIME I'M GONNA KILL IT!!!!

OOOOOOOOOOOOOHHHHHHMMMMMMMMMMMMM...
OK ENOUGH!
TWO MORE OHMS THEN LET'S GO TO MICKEY D'S!!

L-L-L-L-LIKED IT B-B-B-BETTER WHEN U WERE A COU-COU-COUCH P-P-P-P-P POTATO!

LORD!
DON'T MAKE HER A VEGAN!!

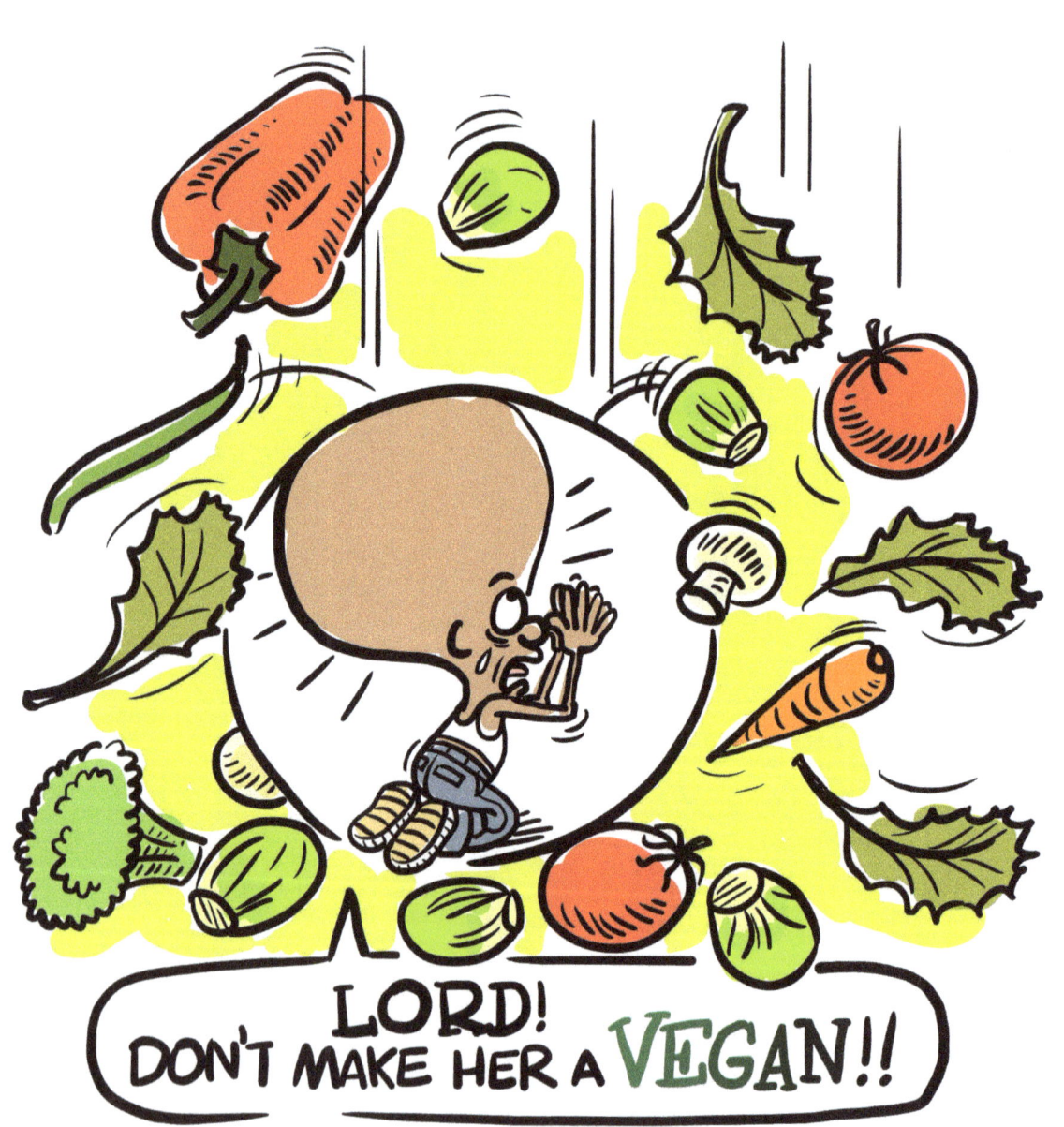

YES!!!!
THAT GOT OVER
A HUNDRED
INGREDIENTS!
SO YOU KNOW YOU
GETTING YOUR
MONEY'S
WORTH!!

9.99
ALL YOU CAN EAT BUFFET $9.99 P.P!
ALL YOU CAN EAT BUFFET 9.99 P.P!
I'M NOT A LAWYER BUT TECHNICALLY YOU EATIN' FOR 2...

TACO SMELL
CHILI LOCO TACOS
CHILI CON COLI
STINKY CHEESY TACO
WE SERVE NO VEGGIES
BURRO BARF BURRITOS
MOO MOO PLATTER
COW UDDER BURRITOS
BEAN BONER BURRITOS
ITSA WRAP
PORN TAMALES
AY!AY
I'M READY THIS TIME!

NO! NO! I DIDN'T SAY YOU HAVE A CUT!!

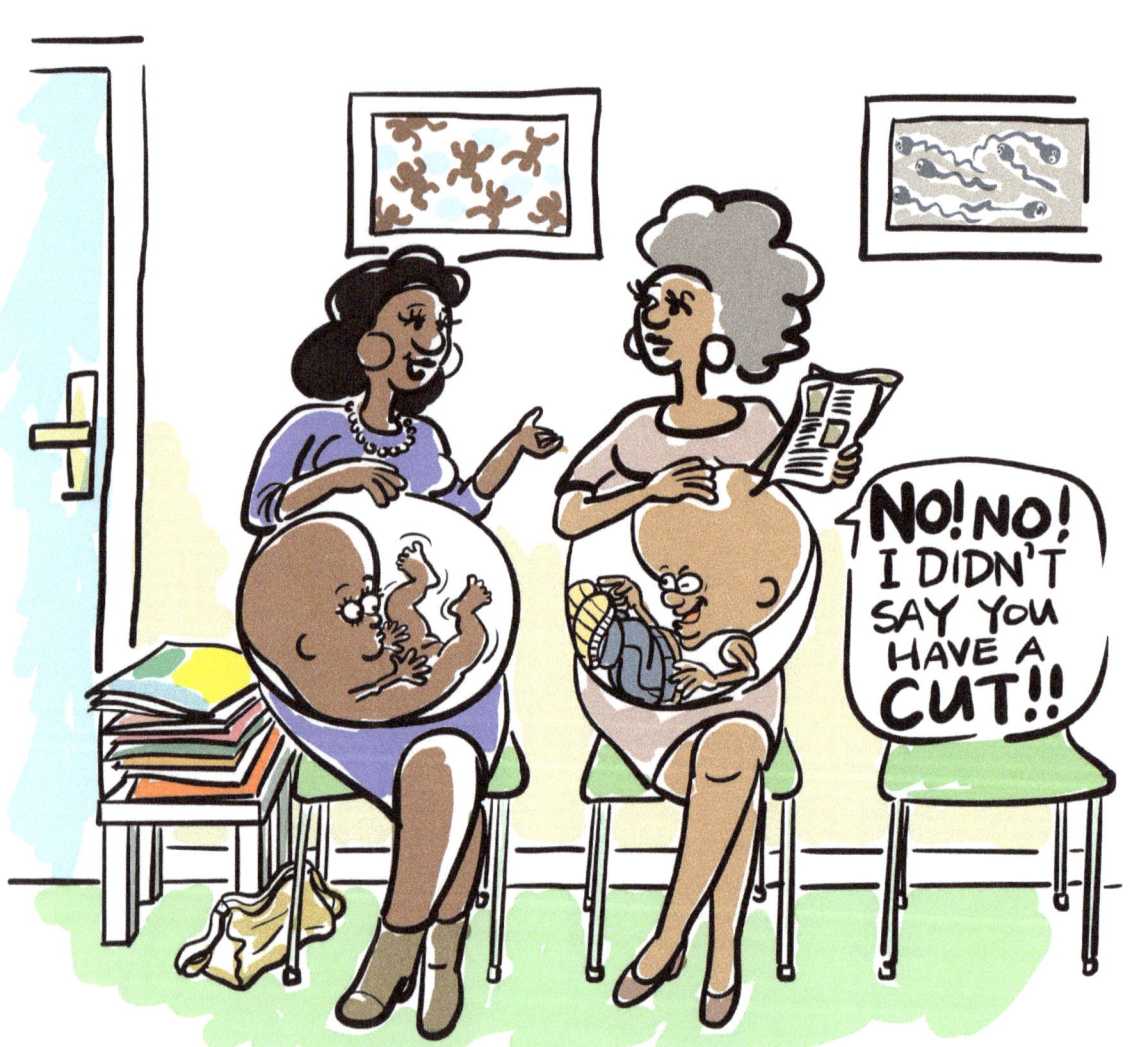

help!
ON
OFF

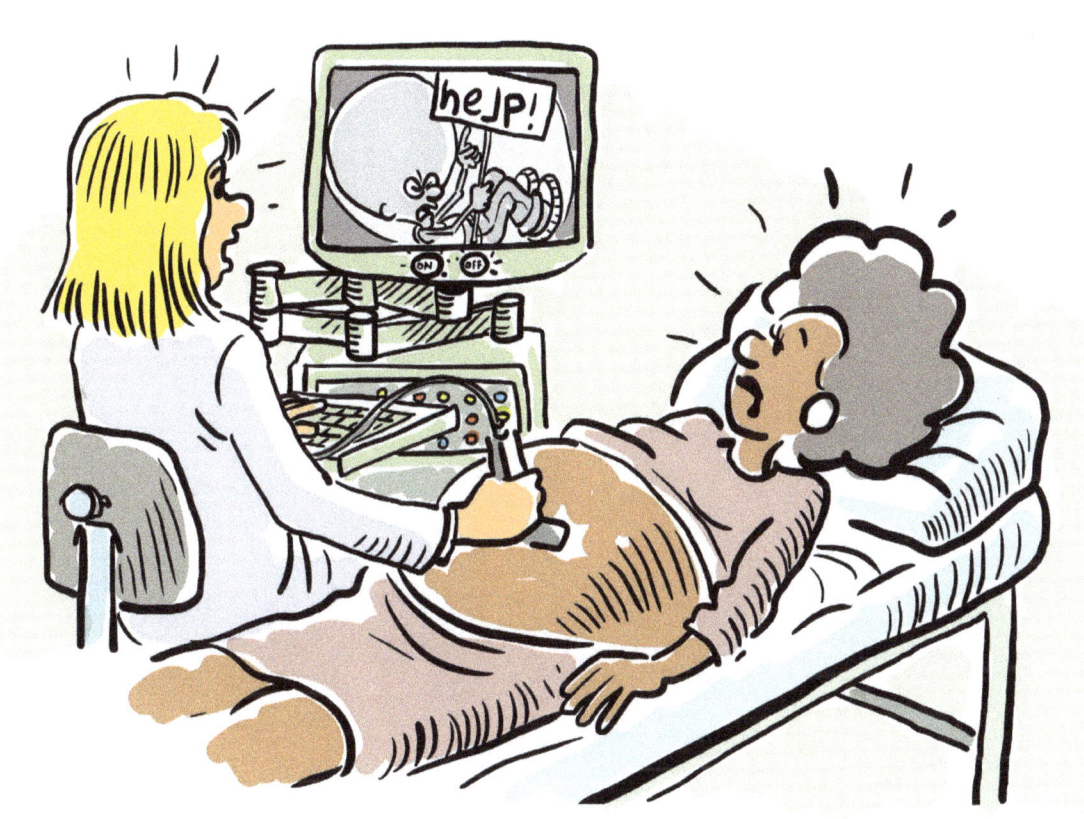

I'M GUESSING THAT AIN'T THE FAMILY PET?

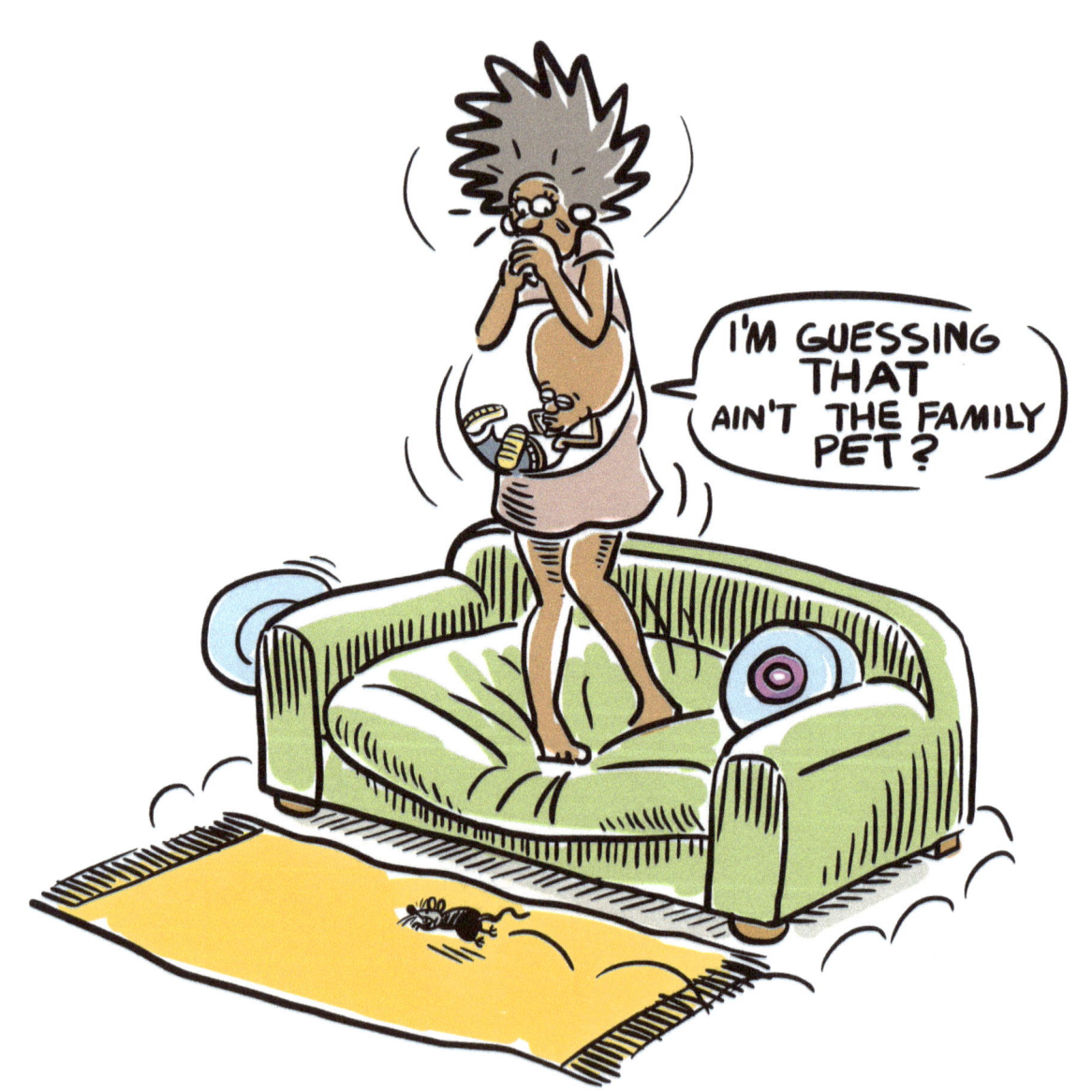

WANNA SEAT?
I'LL BUST A BIG SLOPPY WET ONE AND GET YOU TWO!!

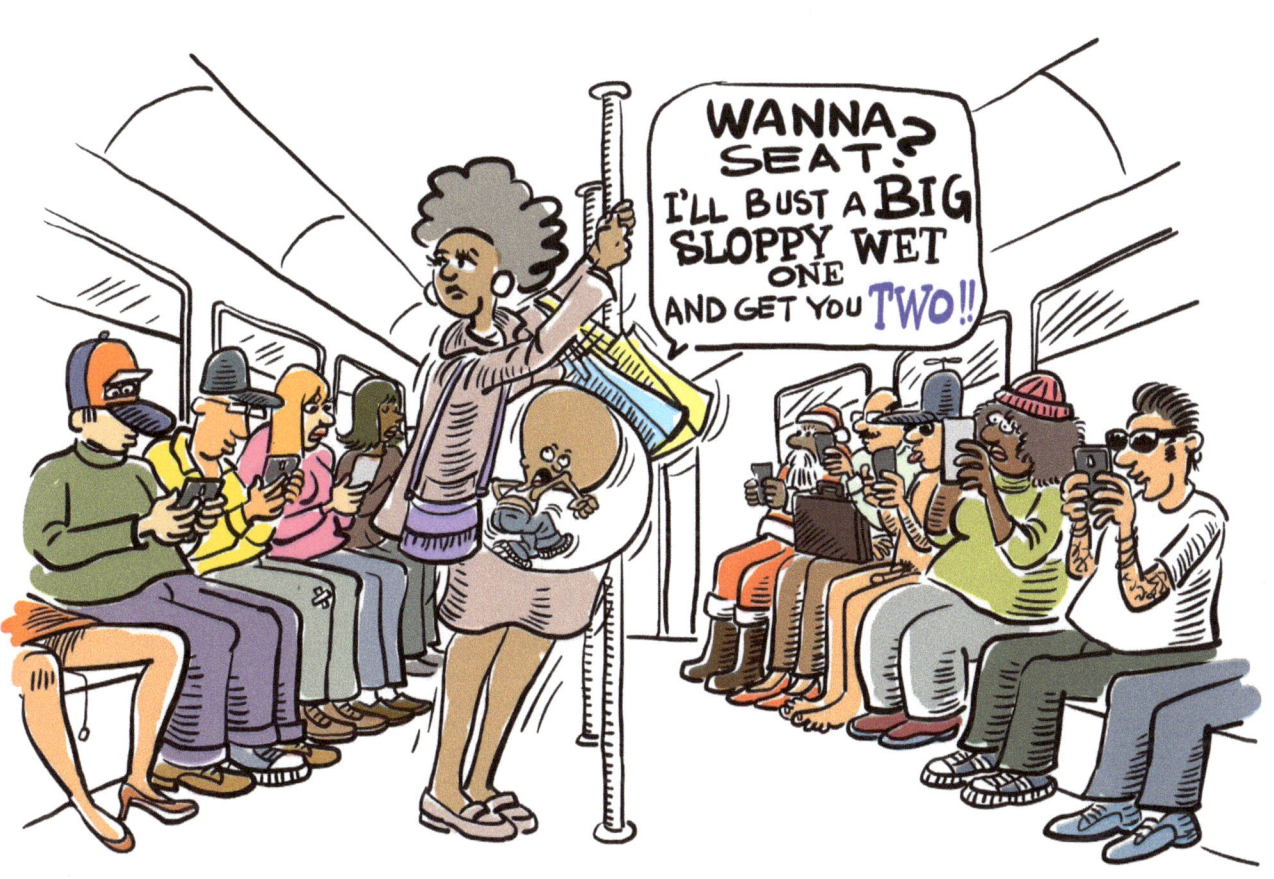

HEY! WE SHOULD MOVE TO COLORADO OPEN A STORE AND SELL KUSH AND CANNABIS GUMMY BEARS!

LOTTERY
LISTEN TO ME! THE POWERBALL IS 8!

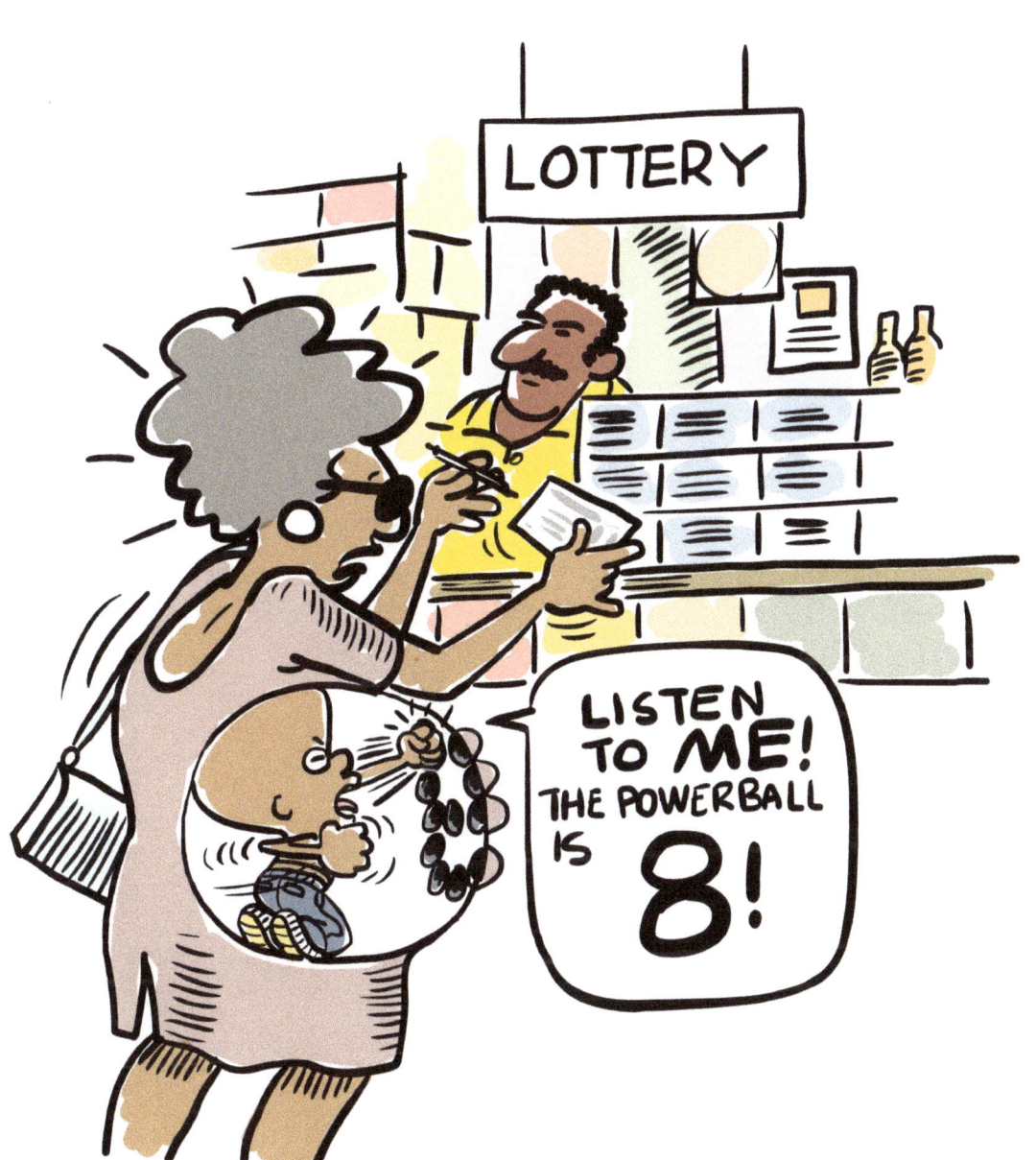

BABY NAMES
R
RANDY
RALPH
RONIN
ROGER
RORY
RONALD
ROPER
ROMAN
REGINALD
REID
YOU KNOW I AIN'T A WHITE BABY RIGHT?

MUSEUM
OF
NATURAL HISTORY
AUSTRALOPITHECUS
DINO
REX
WHO THE F@!!K
WOULD NAME THEIR
KID THAT!

AND THIS TINY LITTLE FO!!!KING BEDROOM WOULD BE FOR WHO?

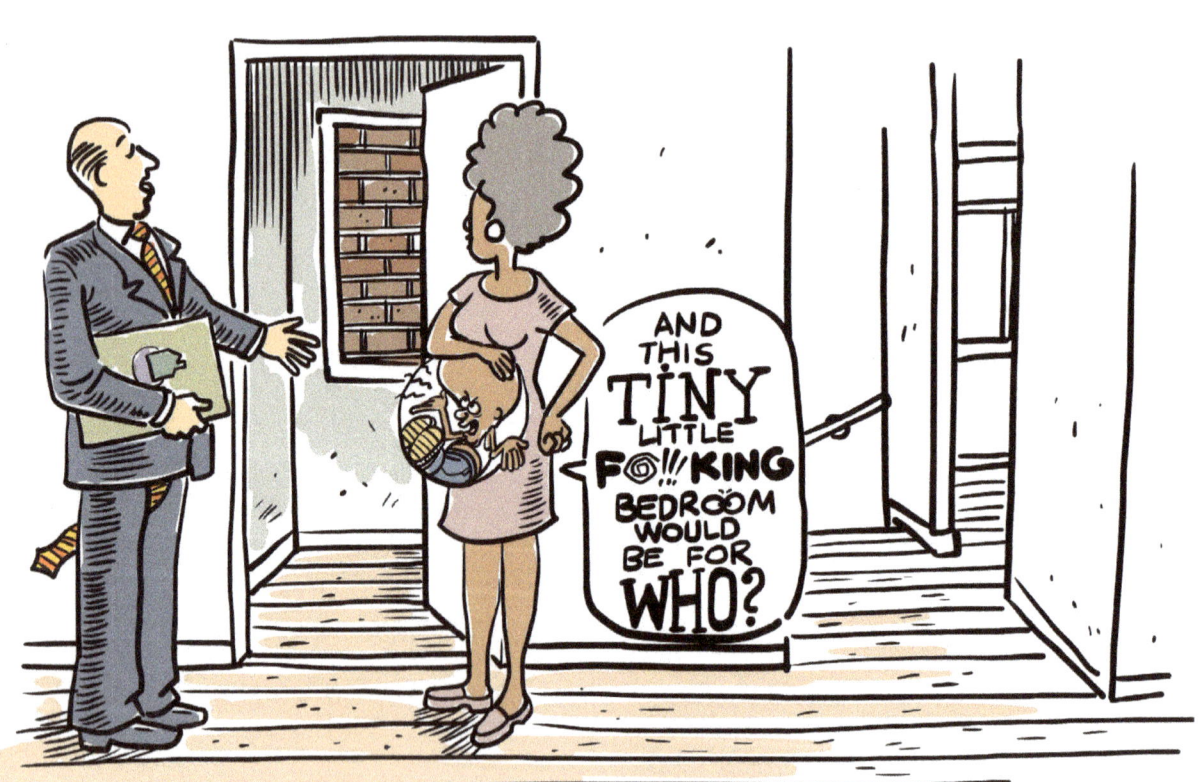

YO! THIS BETTER NOT BE MY S#!T!!!

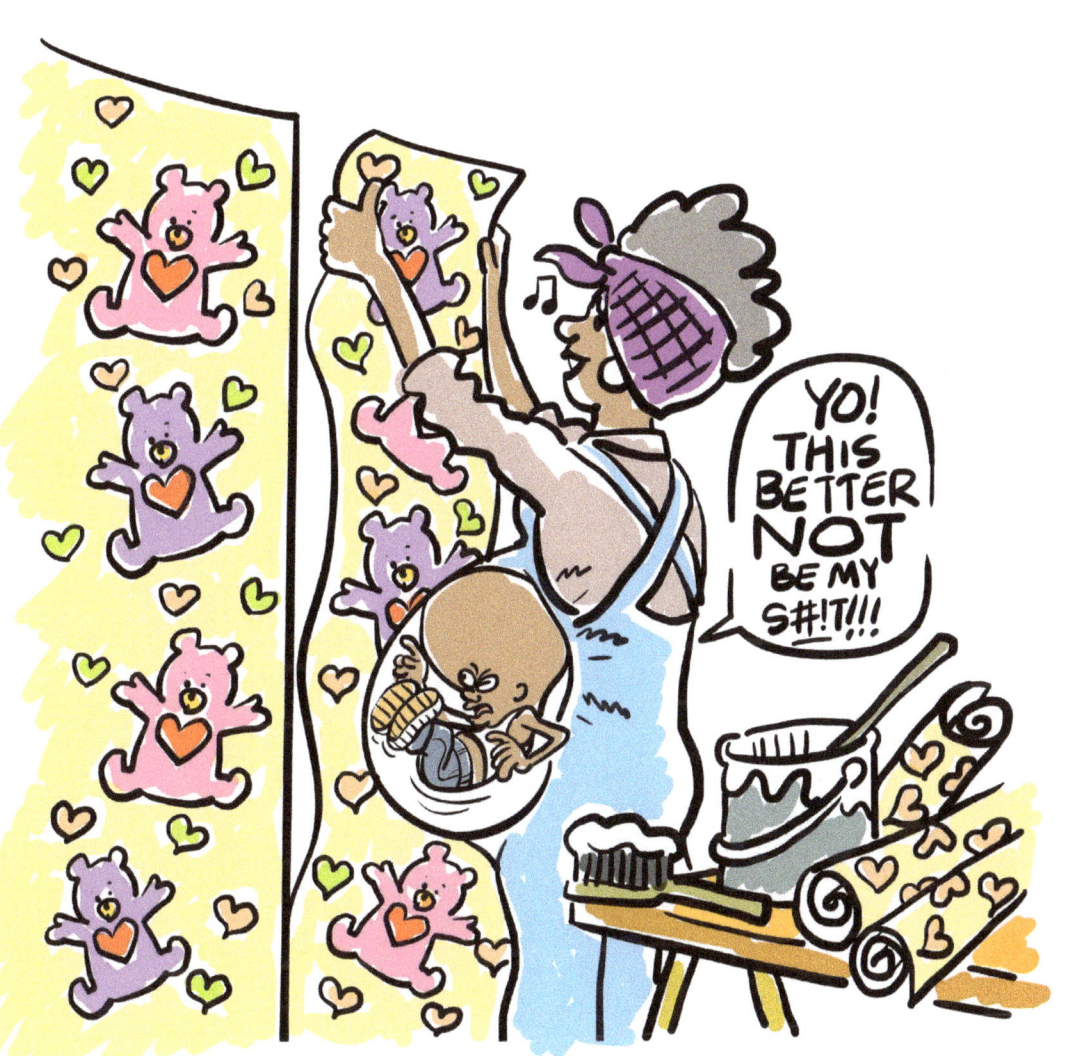

HERE'S MY CELL NUMBER..
I KNEW IT! I'M IN JAIL!
LOAN OFFICER

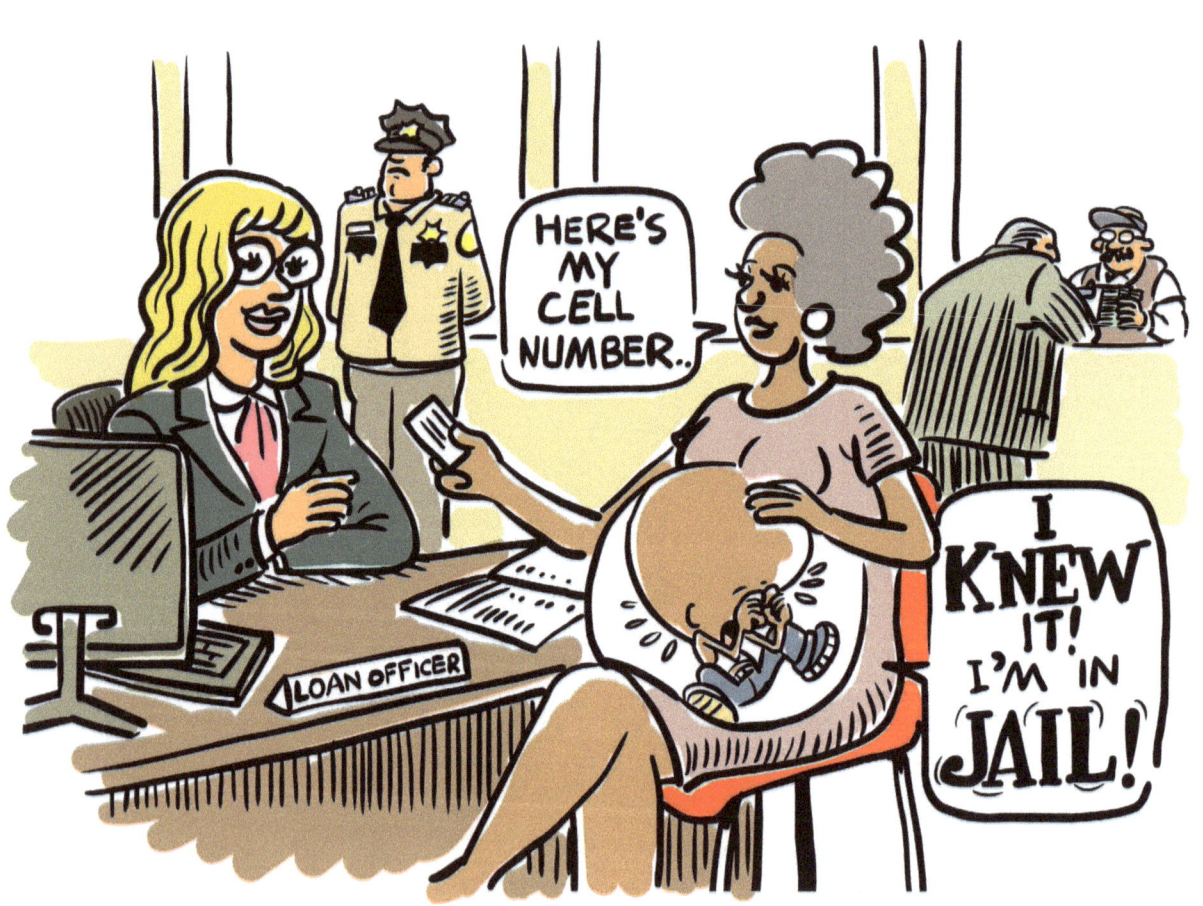

BLACK FRIDAY SALE
HEY! CAN'T YOU WHITE PEOPLE READ??? IT'S BLACK FRIDAY!

NO, NO, THAT DOESN'T MAKE YOU LOOK FAT... AT ALL!!!

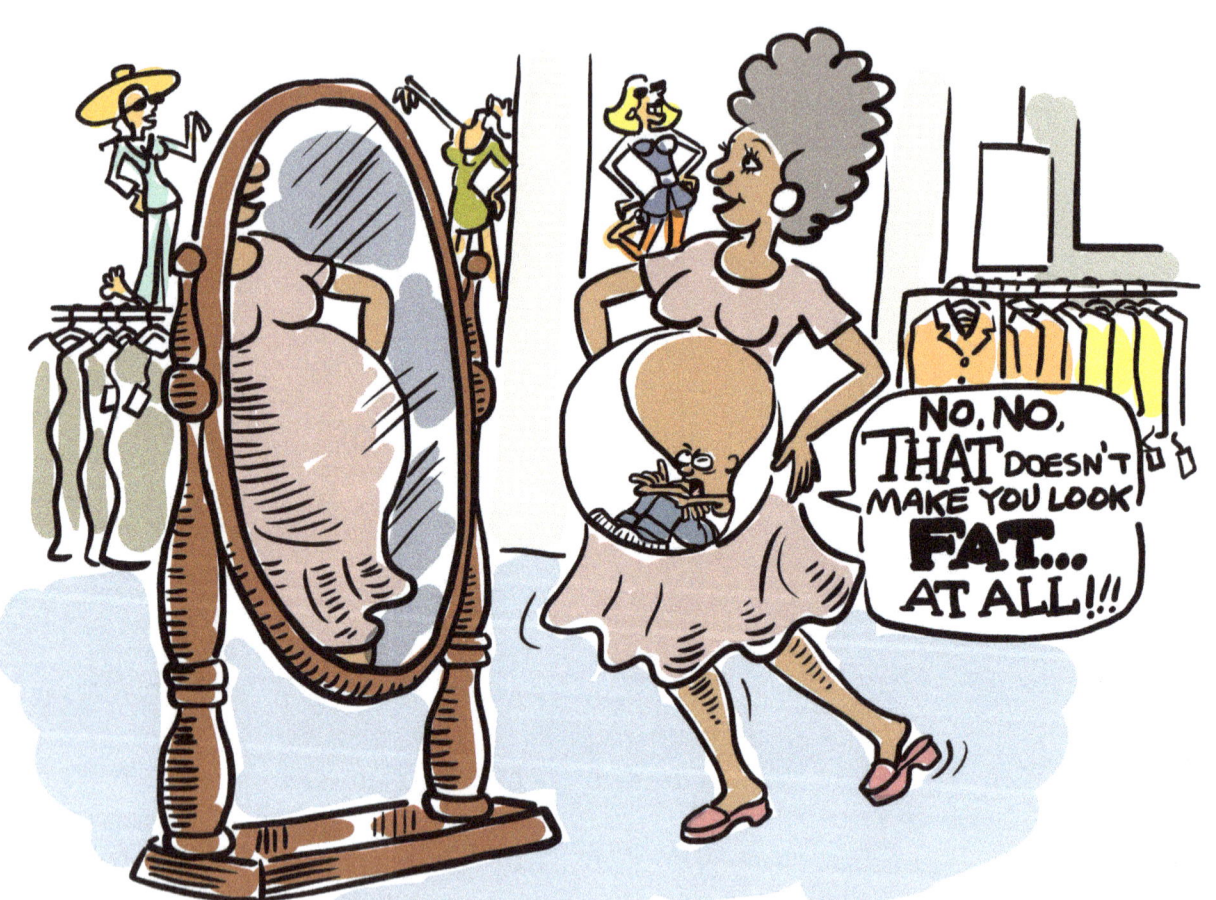

BUT, UH ARE YOU SURE?
LEMME HANDLE THIS MOMMA...
...WHERE WERE YOU ON THE NIGHT OF THE 31TST OF DECEMBER!

$%
!!!
CAR REPAIR
$ 5,773
IF I HAD A NICKEL FOR EVERY TIME SHE SAID "COCKSUCKER."

Y'ALL SHUT
BWAAHAAAAHAB
AMERICAN BABY
FAMILY FUN

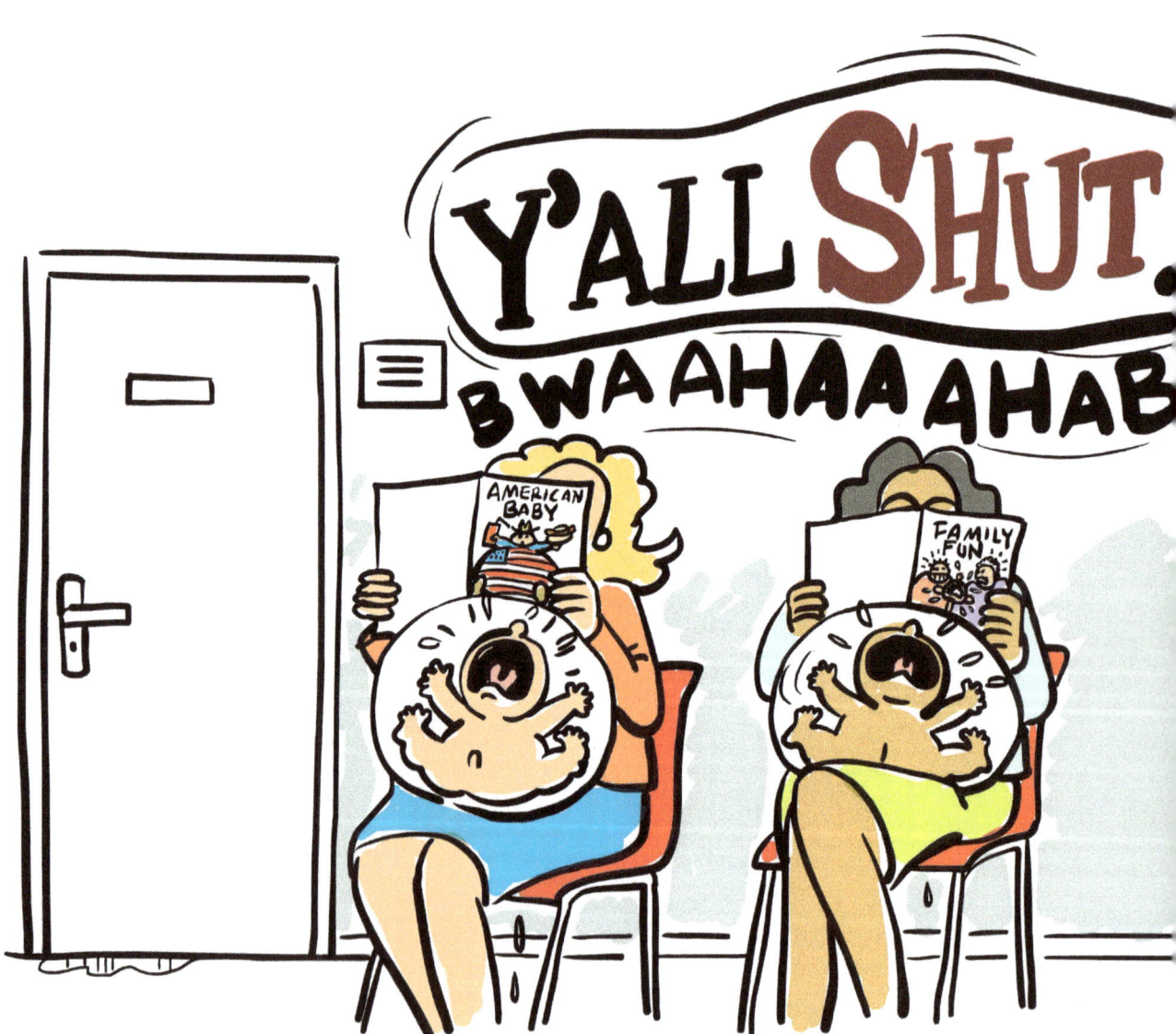

..THE...F#%@☠K...UP!
HAHA
AAAAABWAAAHH!!
BABY YOLK
SMOTHERING
FIT PREG NANCY

ROAR!!!
I THINK I JUST SHIT OURSELVES!

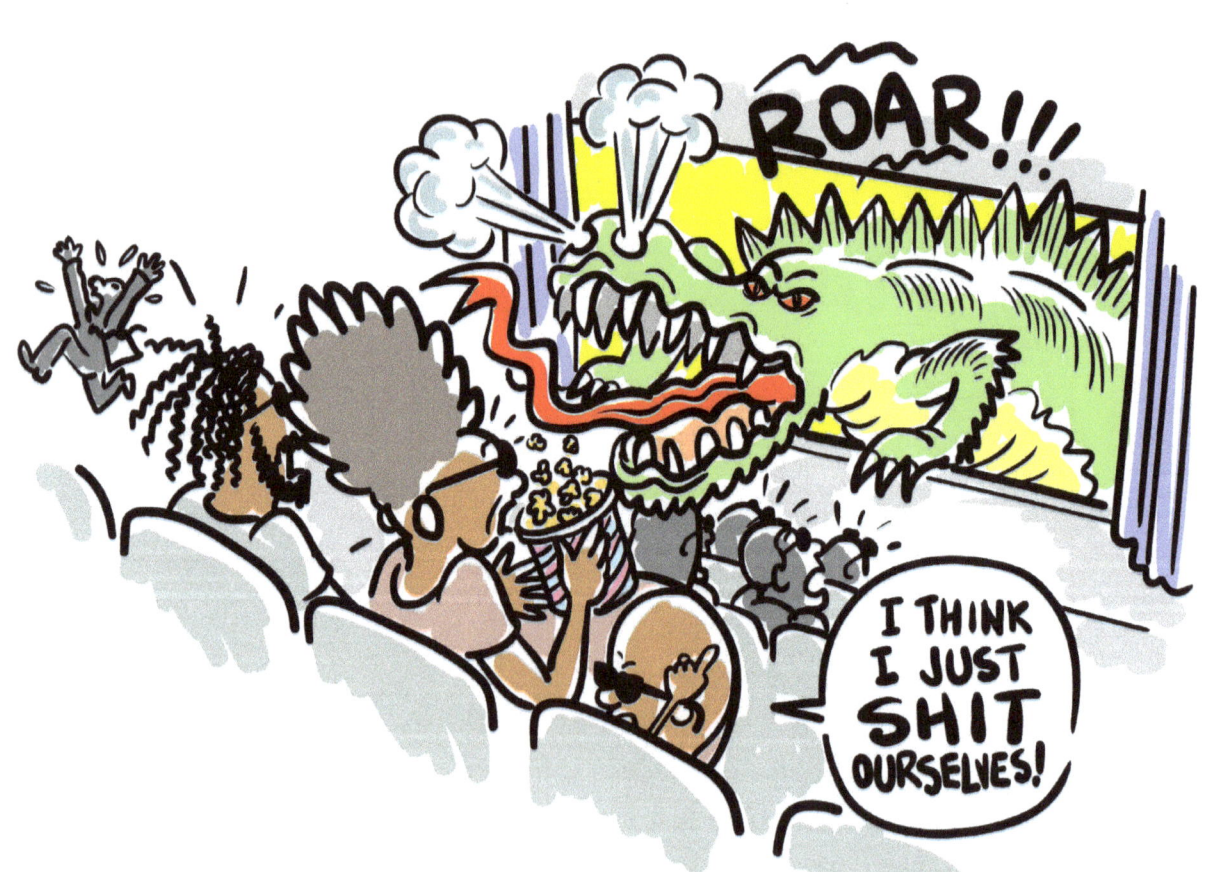

OH YEAH, WANT REAL THRILLS? THEN GET READY TO GIVE BIRTH THROUGH YOUR MOUTH!

I DON'T GIVE A F*K IF IT'S YOUR 25TH BIRTHDAY
GIIIIIIIIIIIIIIIIIIIIIIIIIFT!! I-I-I-I AYYYYYYYYEEEEEEEEEEEEEEEE

STOP
I'LL TALK
NO MORE
WATER BOARDING!!

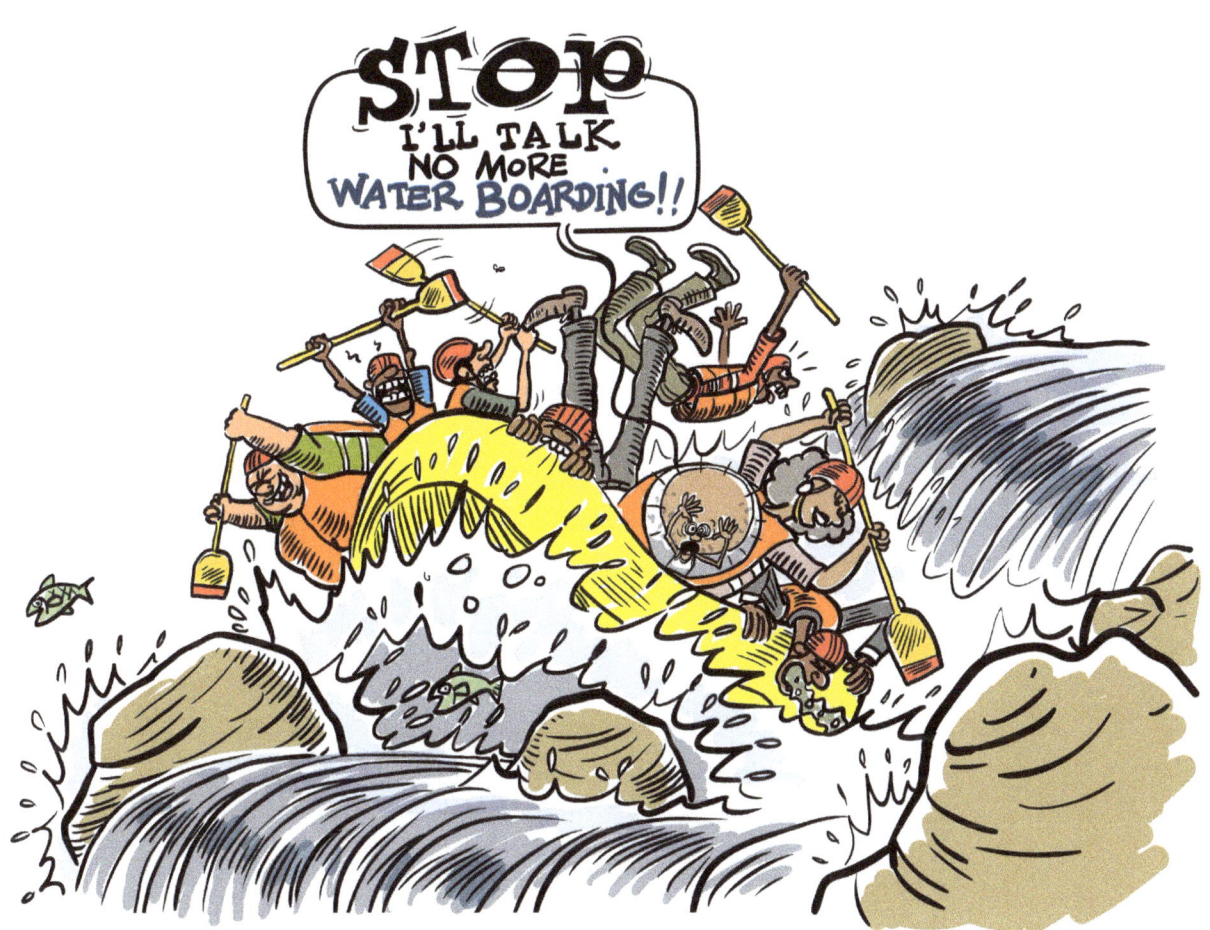

U.S.
HISTORY
HER
ROSA PARKS
YOU SAID WE GOIN' TO THE PARK! WHERE THE SWINGS!

LGBTQ?

THIS DEF' GOIN' UP ON FETUSBOOK!

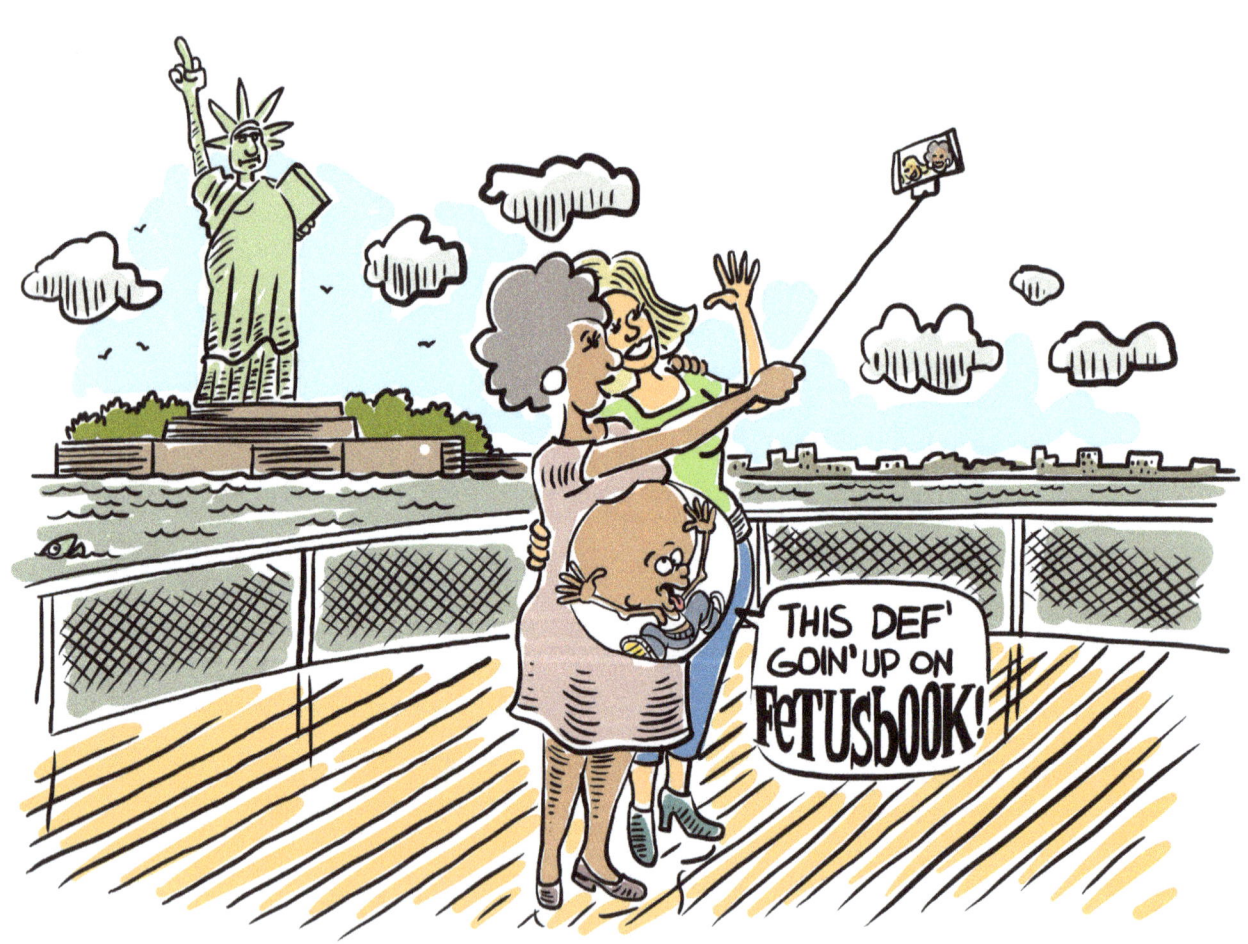

HEEEEEY! EASY HONEY!! THIS AIN'T ALADDIN'S LAMP!

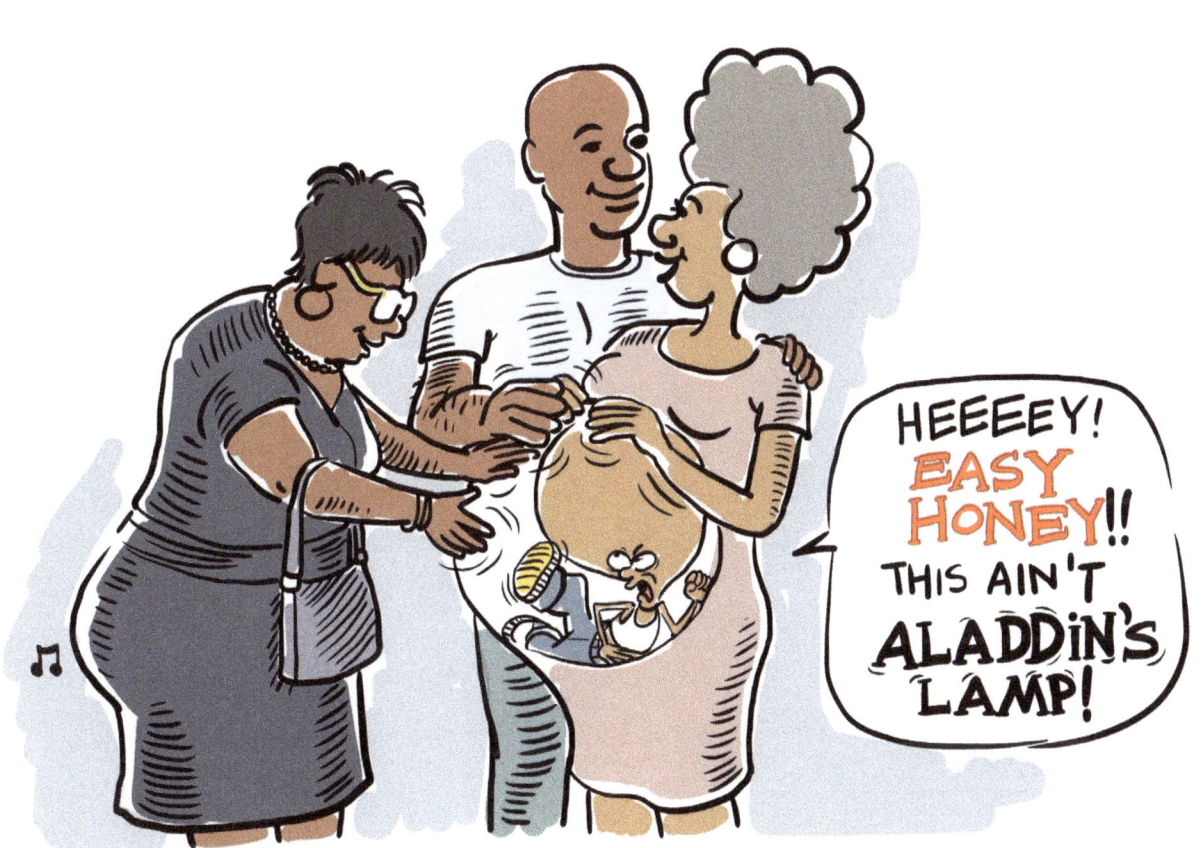

DUKE 1
GONZAGA 0
YOU KNOW YOU'RE GONNA BUST MY BRACKET!

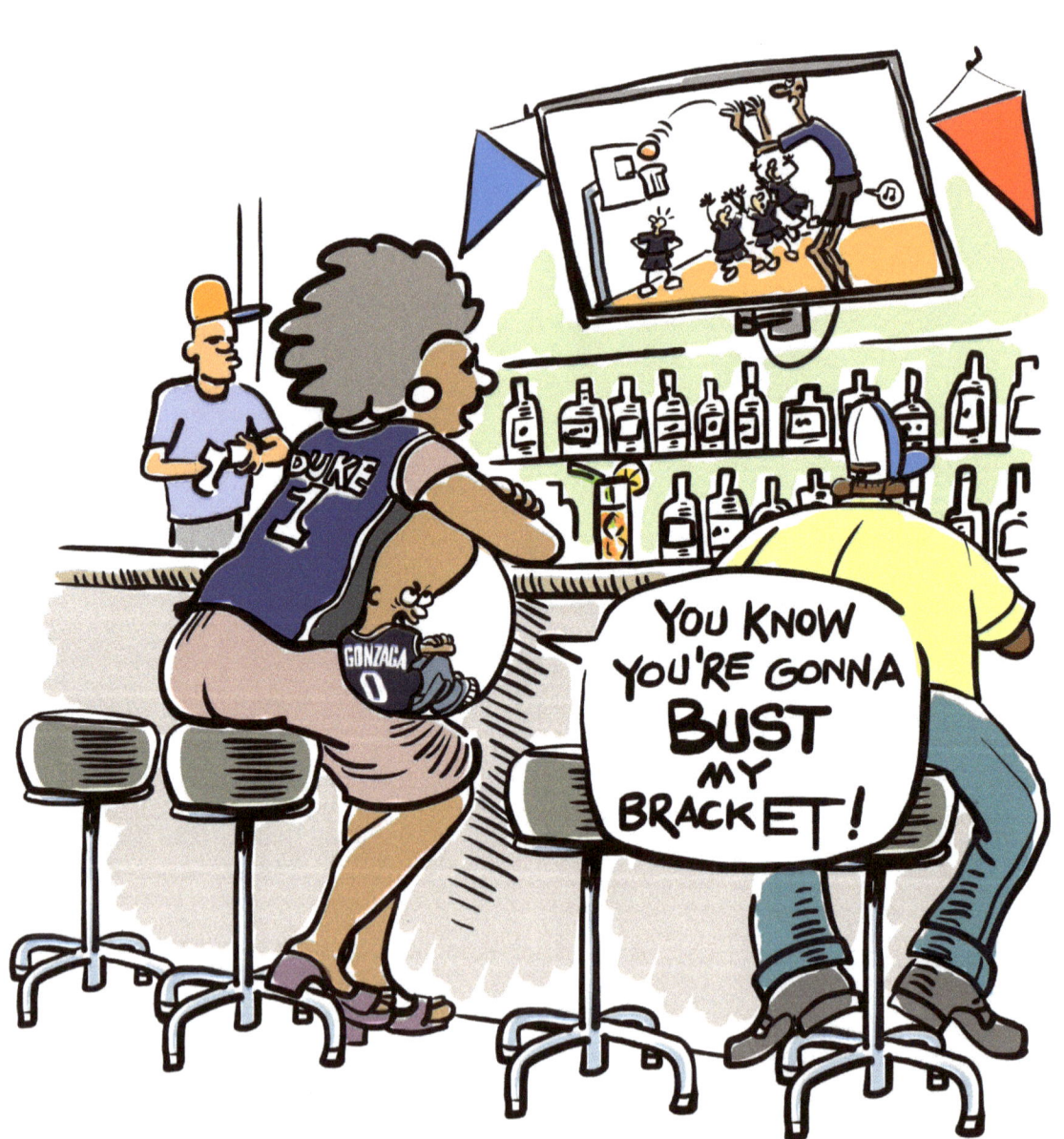

SO A LITTLE ******
AND A BIG ****** WALK INTO A BAR...
DAVE CHAPELLE
MOMMA, WHAT'S A ******?

STOP
BLACK FETUSES MATTER!

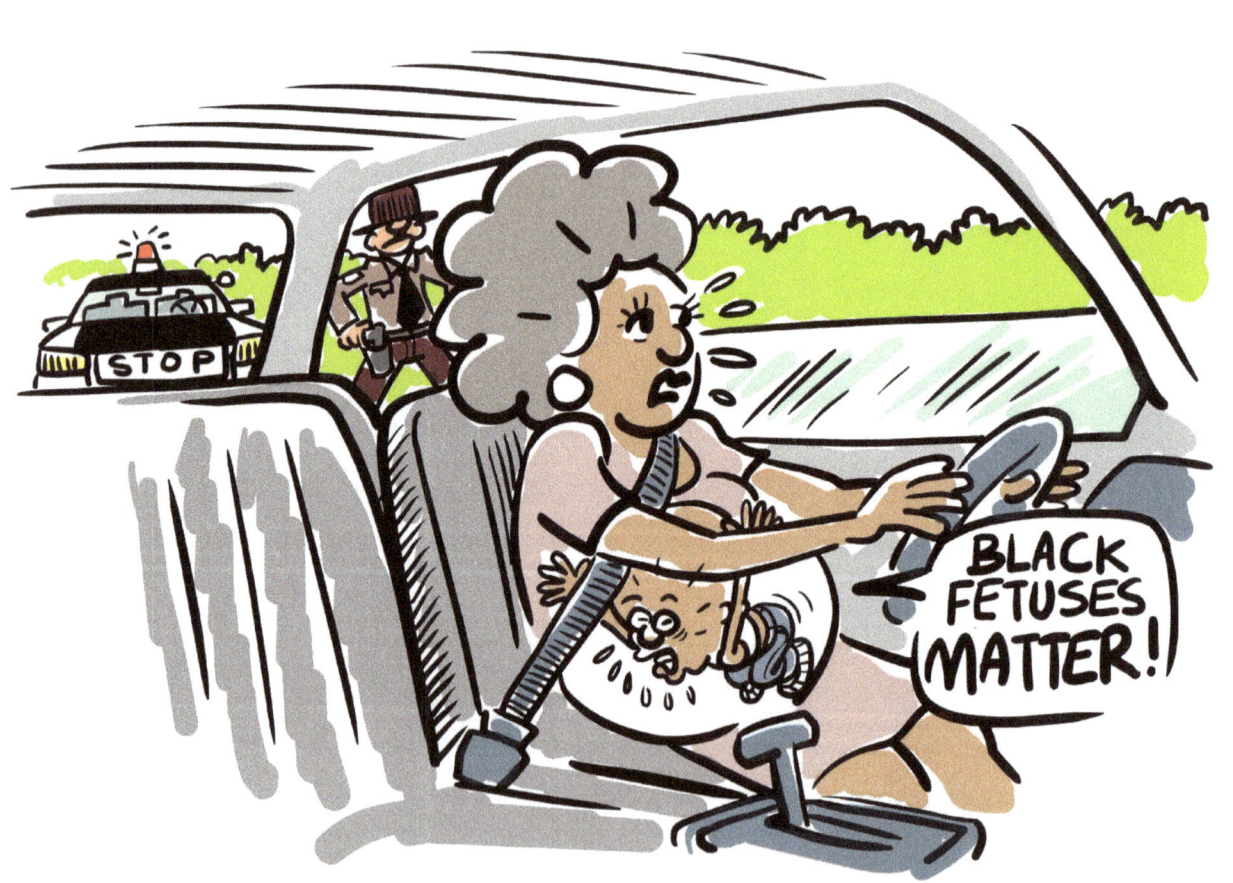

CRACK!
BOOM!
BOOM!
CRACK!
BOOM!
BY STPHEN STORM
REBECCA
DUCK
MOMMA! IT'S A DRIVE BY!!

SOOOO, IF YOU LOVE ME SO MUCH WHY'D YOU EAT ME??

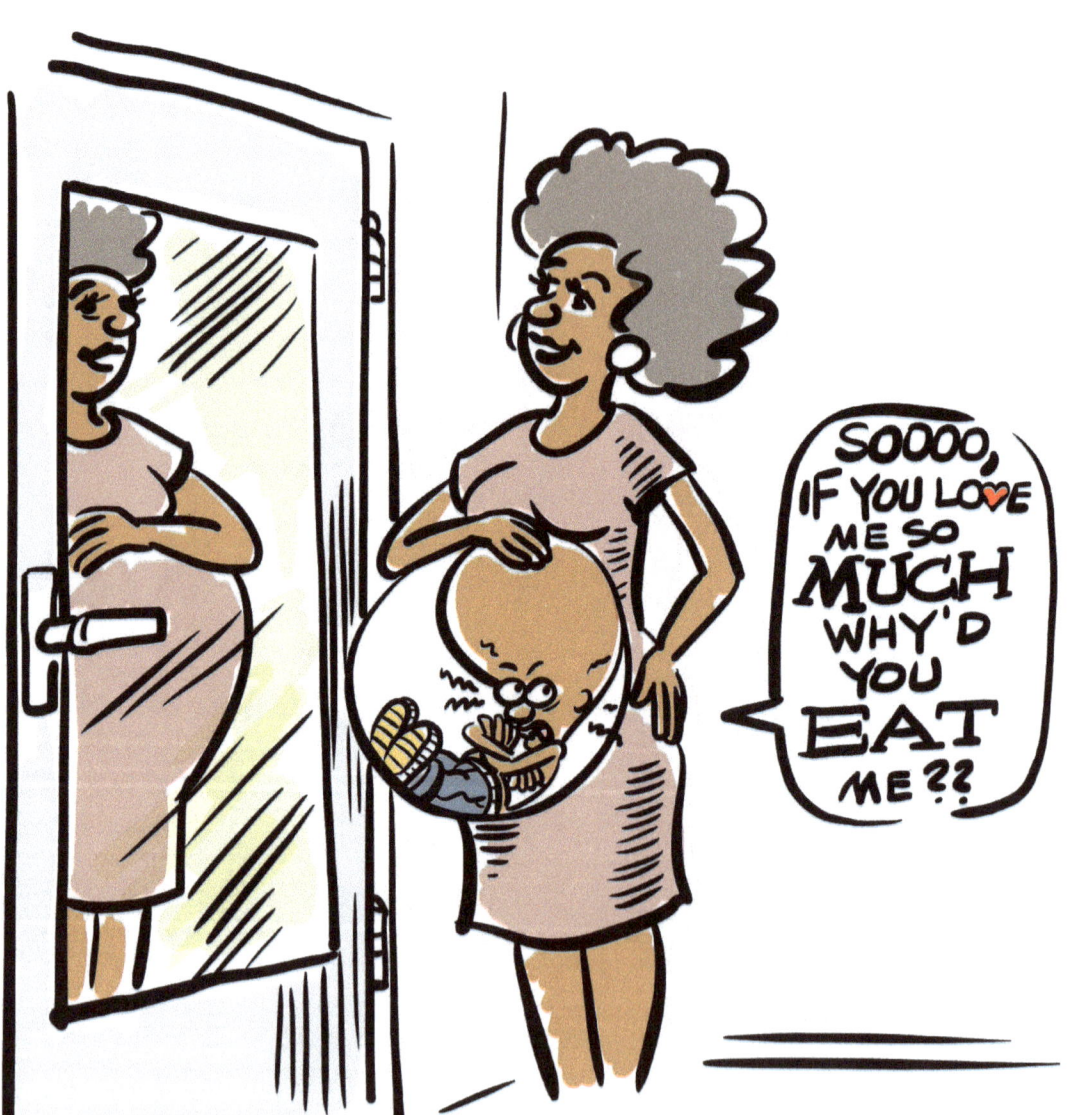

YO!! HIT ME UP WHEN YOU GET OUT BABE, I'D LIKE TO SOIL YOUR DIAPER!!

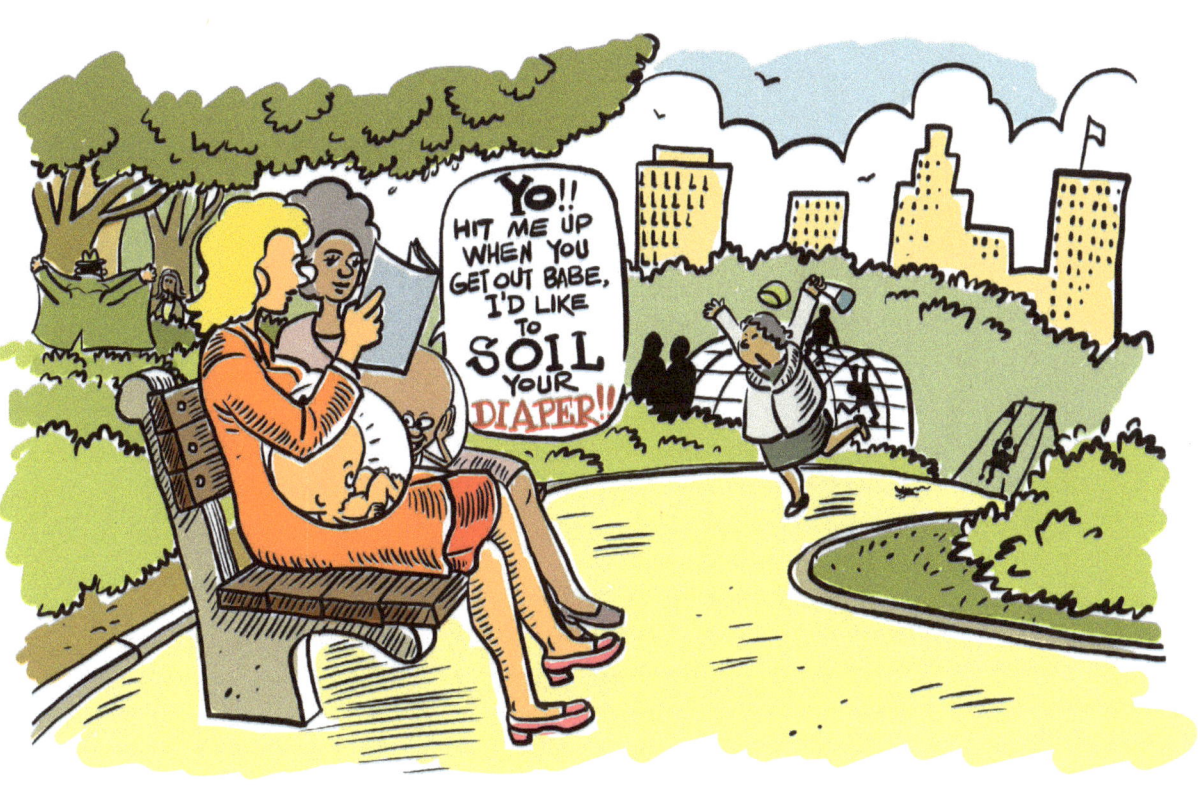

AM I SUPPOSED TO FEED YOU PET YOU, OR WHAT?

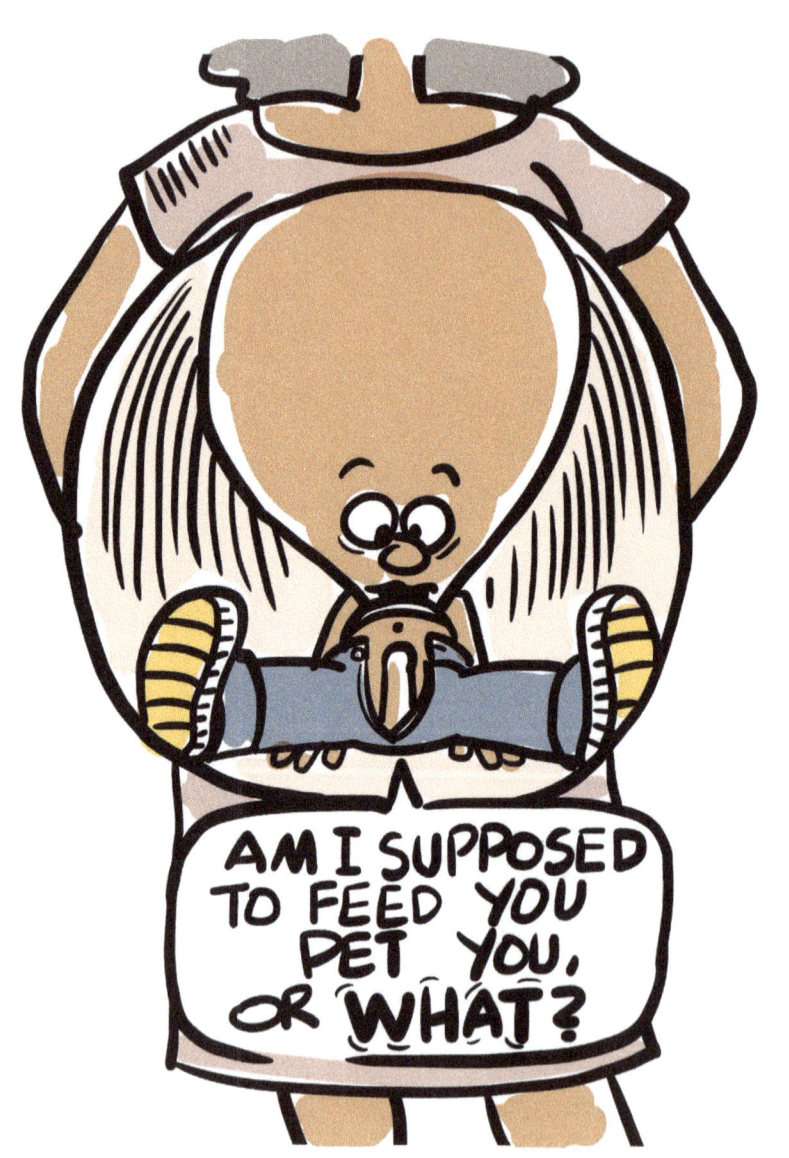

TRY THIS S#IT ONE MORE TIME I'M GONNA YANK YOU THE FO!!!K OUT!

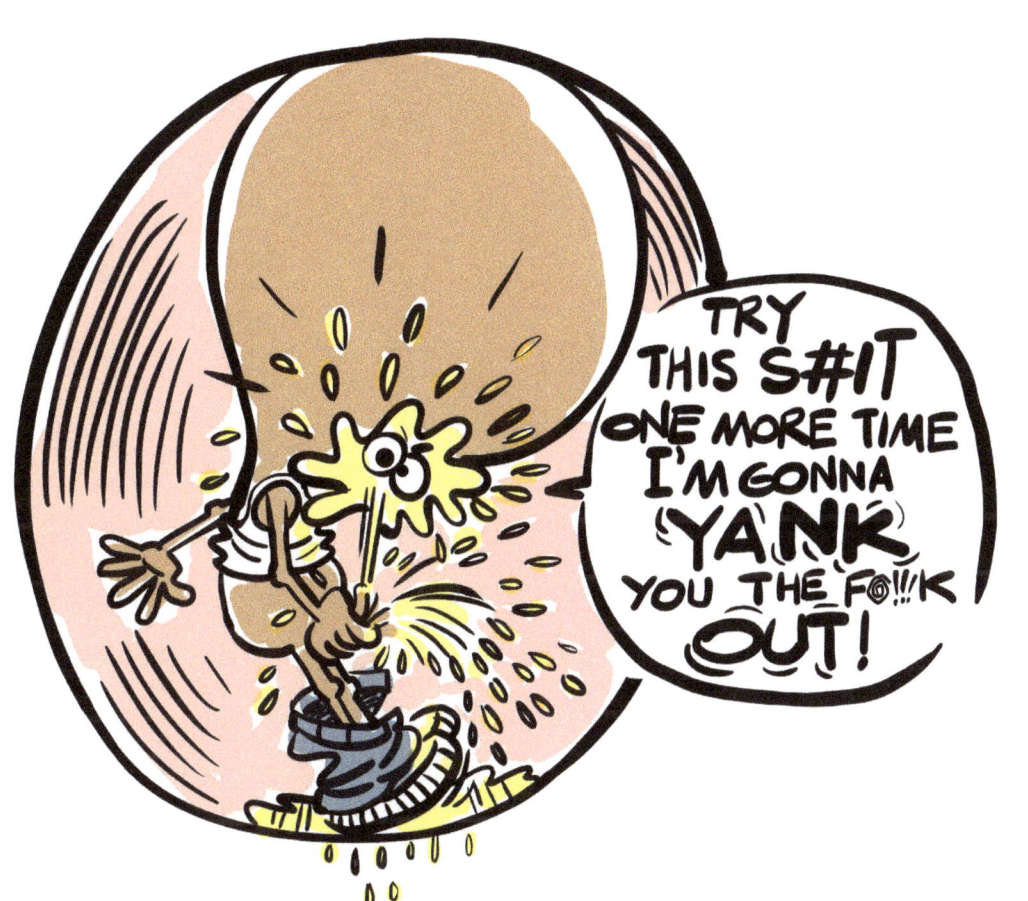

TWIN PEAKS
THRILLDREN
MAMA POPPA MAMA MOMMA PAPA MAMA MAMA PAPA PAPA PAPA
YOU DUDES GONNA MAKE SOME SERIOUS COIN IN THE CIRCUS!

9-1-1! THERE'S A 10-62 IN PROGRESS!

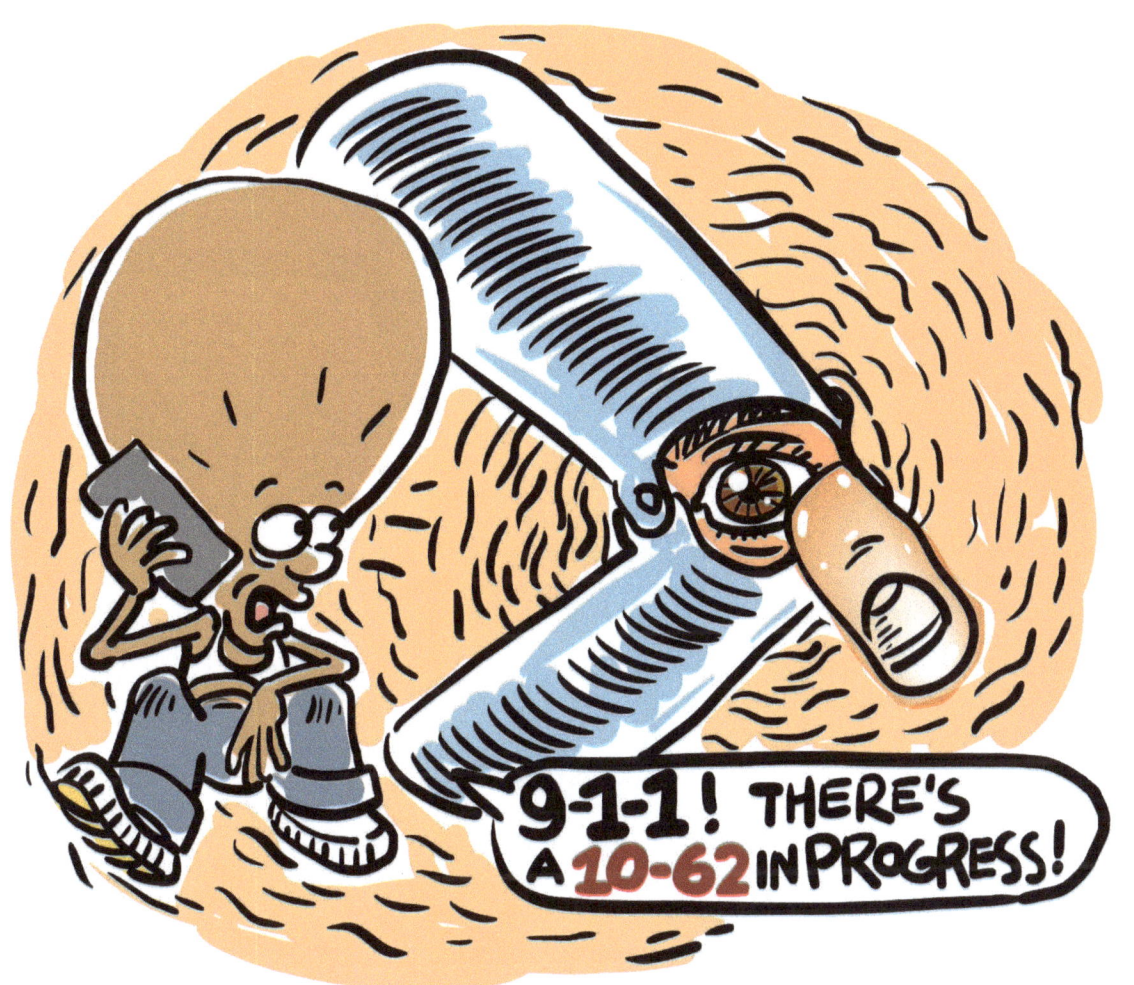

JESUS CHRIST! THAT MUSTA HURT!!

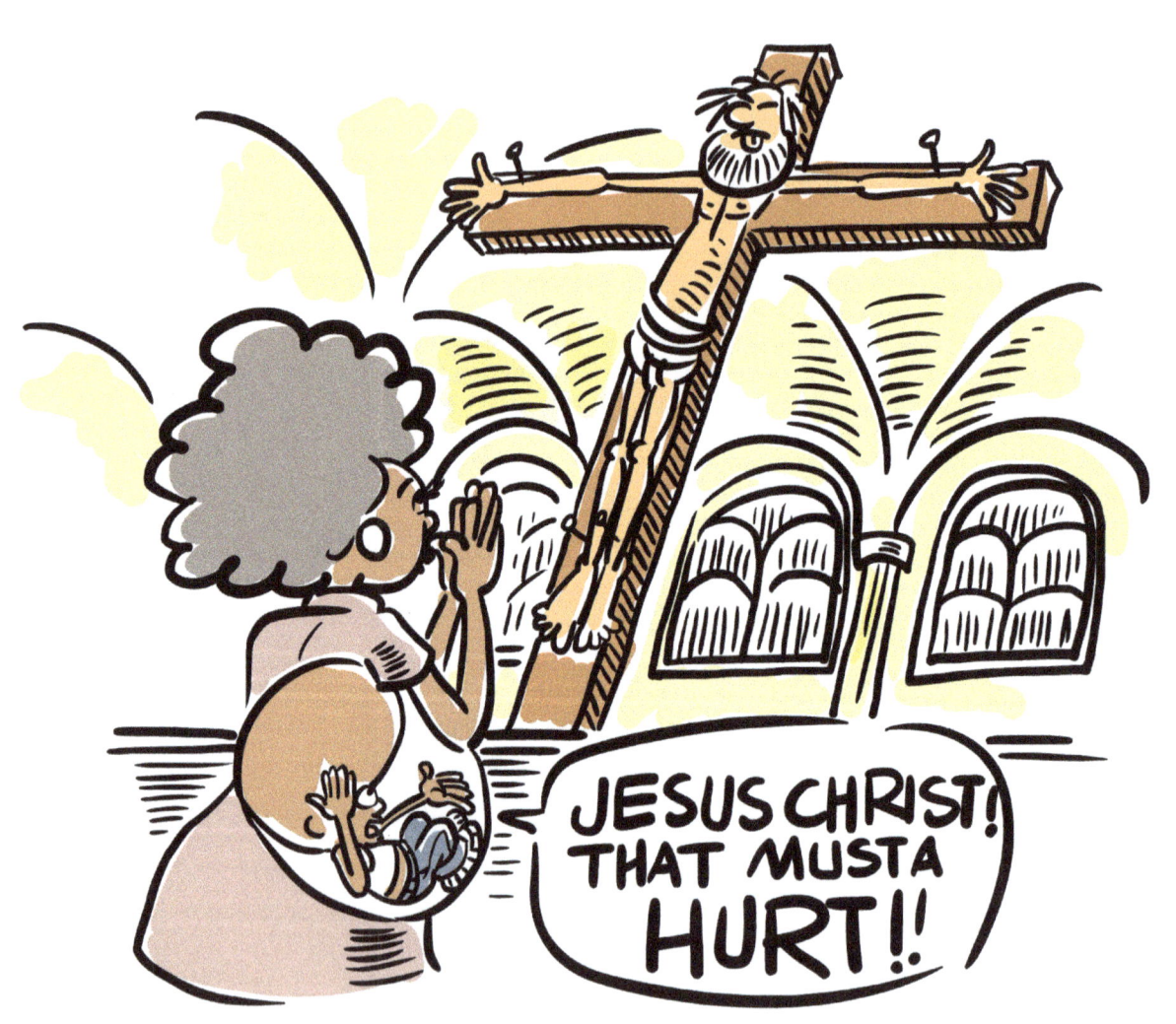

I REFUSE TO BE IN THIS CARTOON!
MORE CHITLINS!

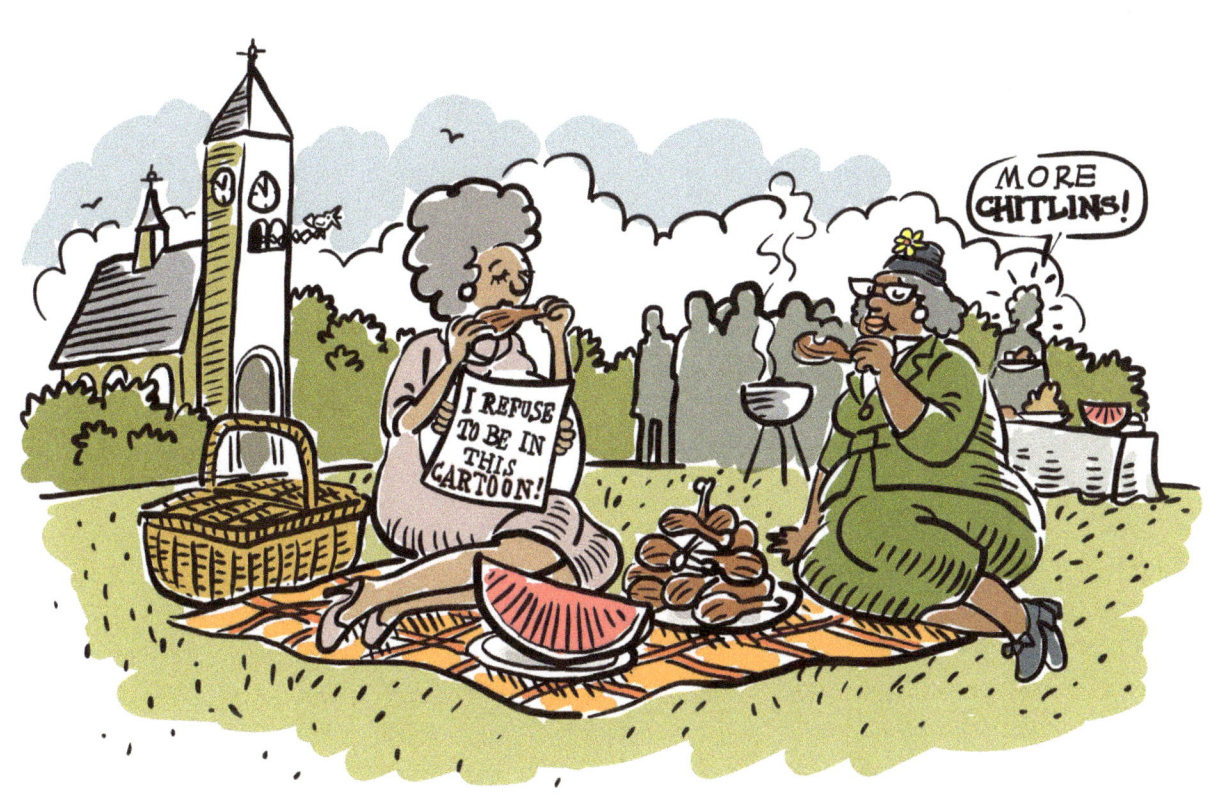

I'M DREAMING
OF A...
BLACK CHRISTMAS!

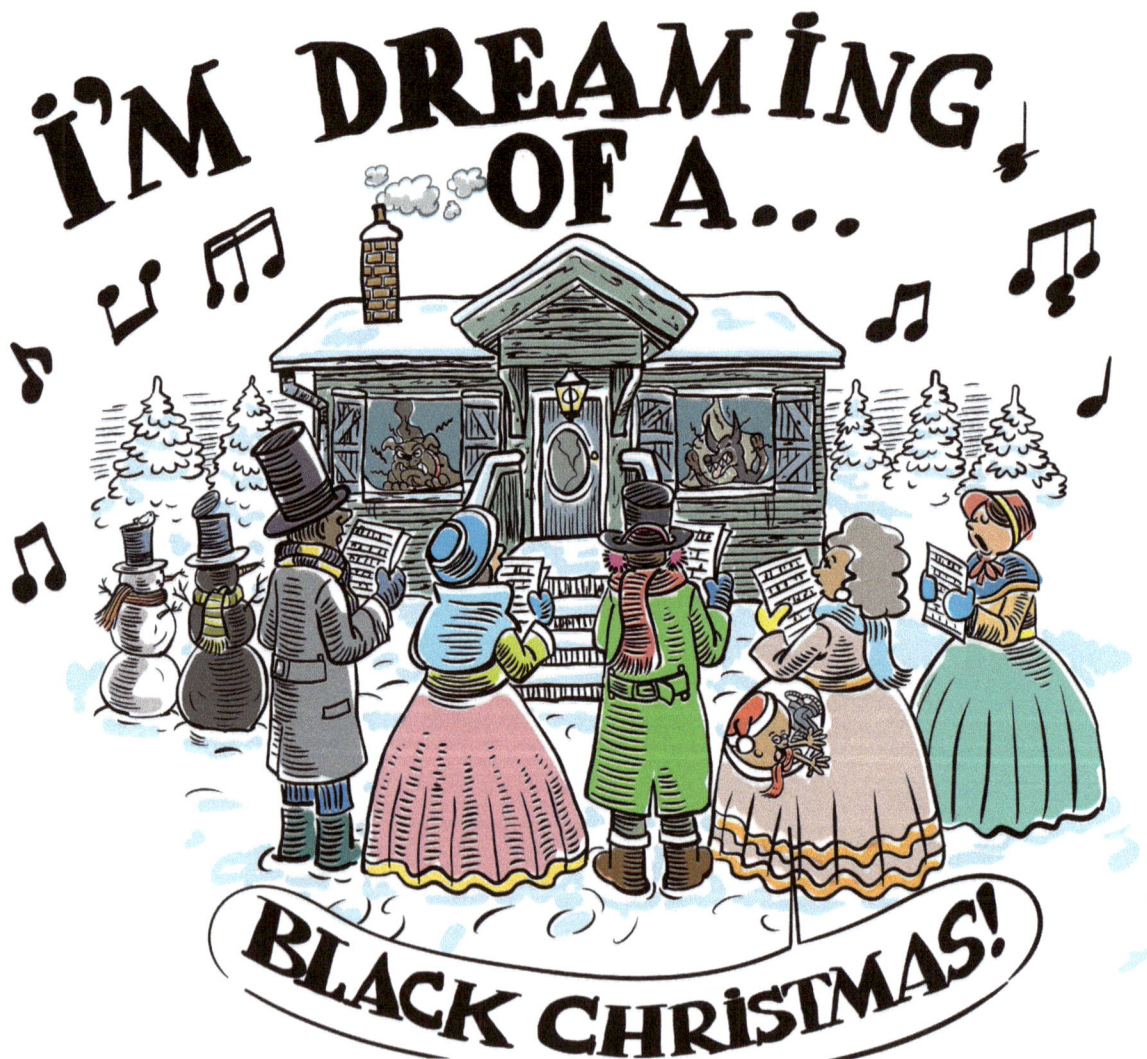

YO! YO! YO! MERRY XMAS Y'ALL!
I TOLD YOU, NO ANCHOVIES!
NO! NO! NOT TODAY!! MY BIRTHDAYS WILL BE RUINED FOREVER!!

SO, UH... WHAT'S THE EXIT STRATEGY?

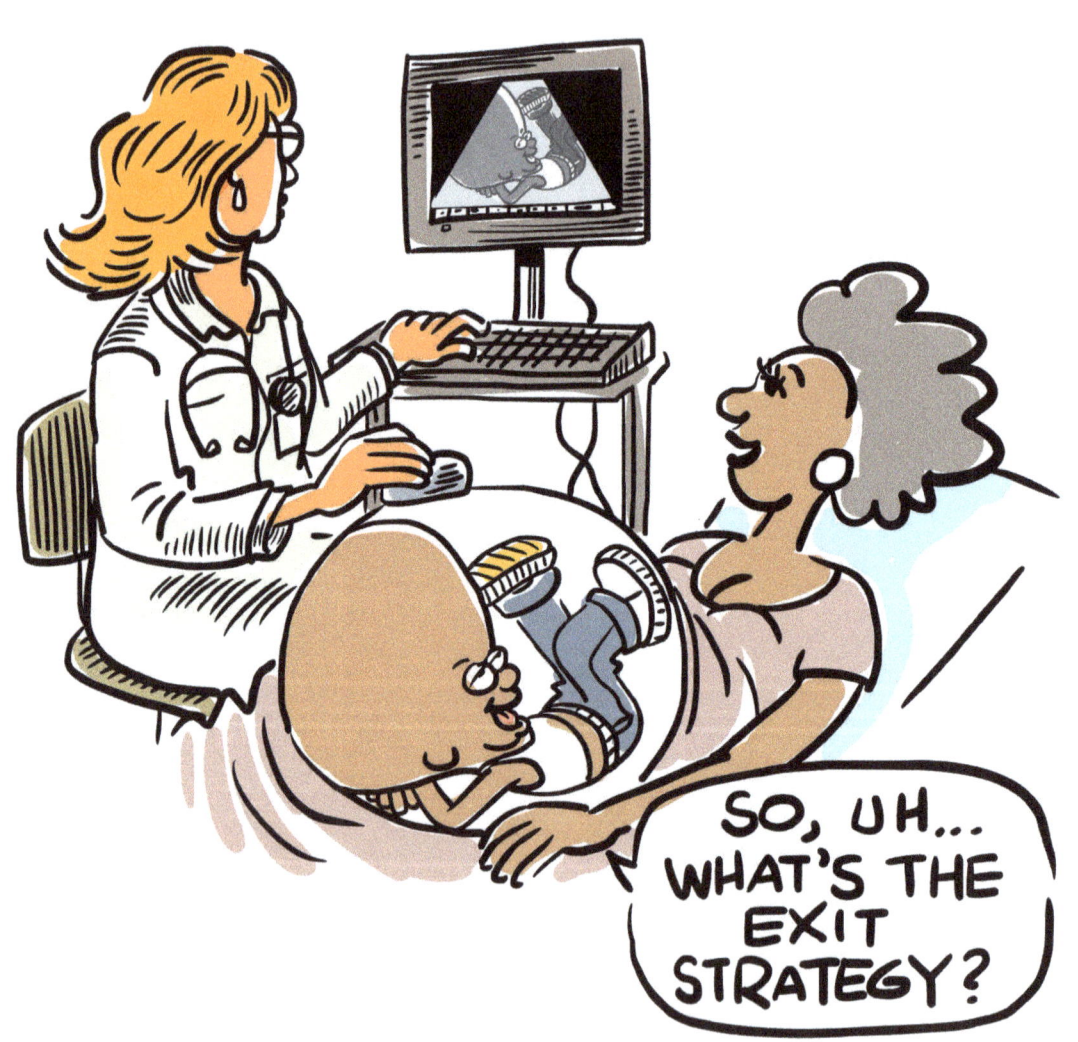

POWERBALL
JACKPOT IS NOW
$1000
MILLION
17
YOU TOLD HIM
YOU'RE PLAYING
YOUR DUE DATE?
TH-TH-THATS....
TOMORROW!!

FISHBONE GRILL
FETUS OVERBOARD!

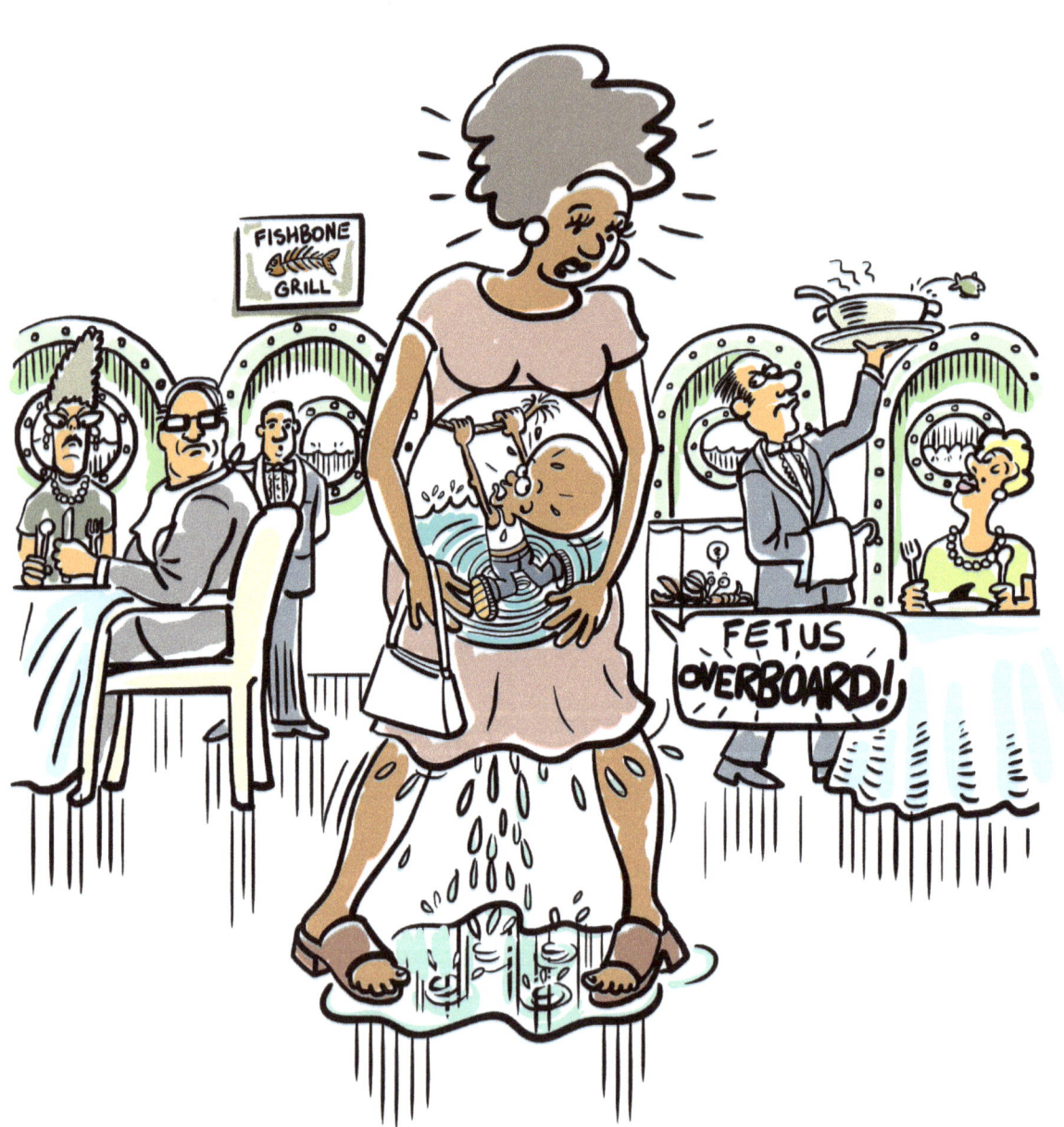

menu
ON
OFF
OH!
OMG!
SHIT
EHM
U.S. MALE
SPECIAL DELIVERY
KNOCK! KNOCK!
HEY! IF YOU'RE THINKIN' A C-SECTION, DON'T BLAME ME IF I'M A C-STUDENT!

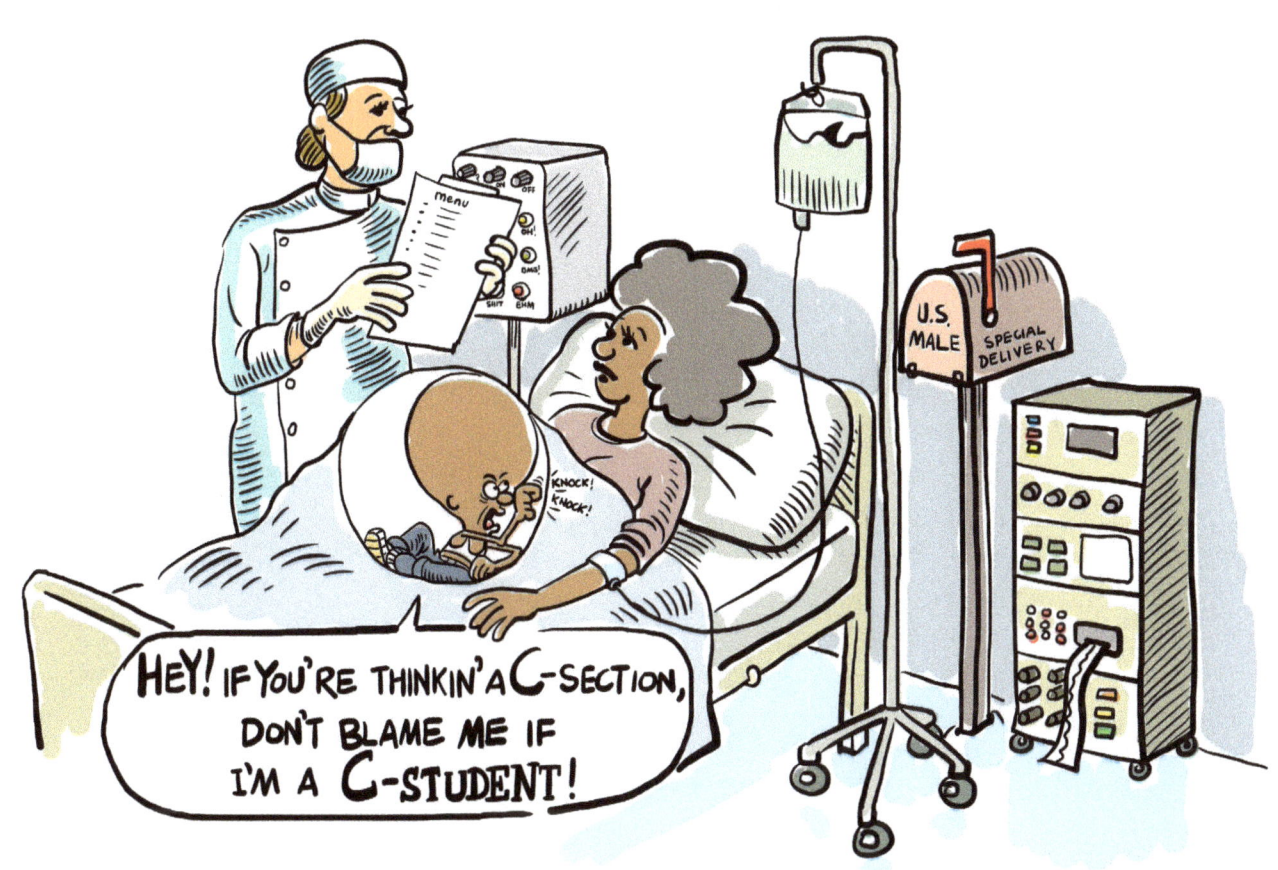

AAAAARRGGGHH!!!
I SWEAR! IT WASN'T ME.
I DIDN'T DO NOTHIN'!!!

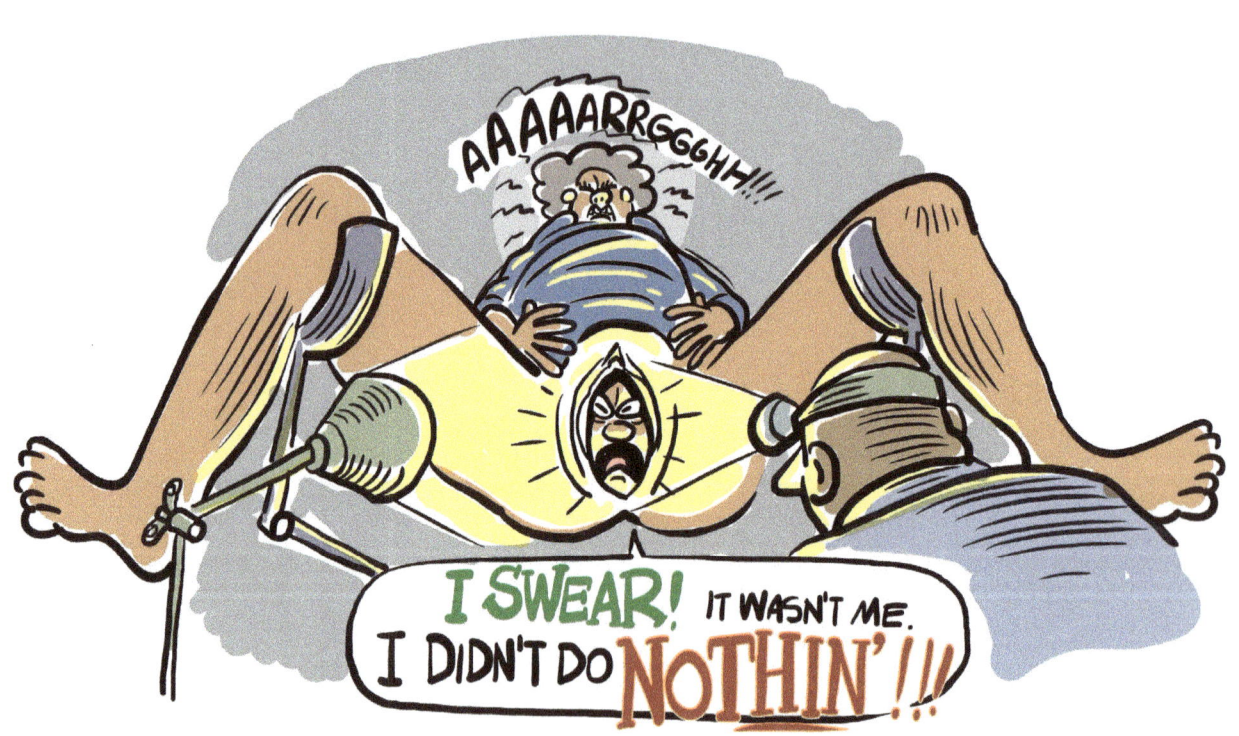

BACK OFF!
MOTHERF#@KERS!!

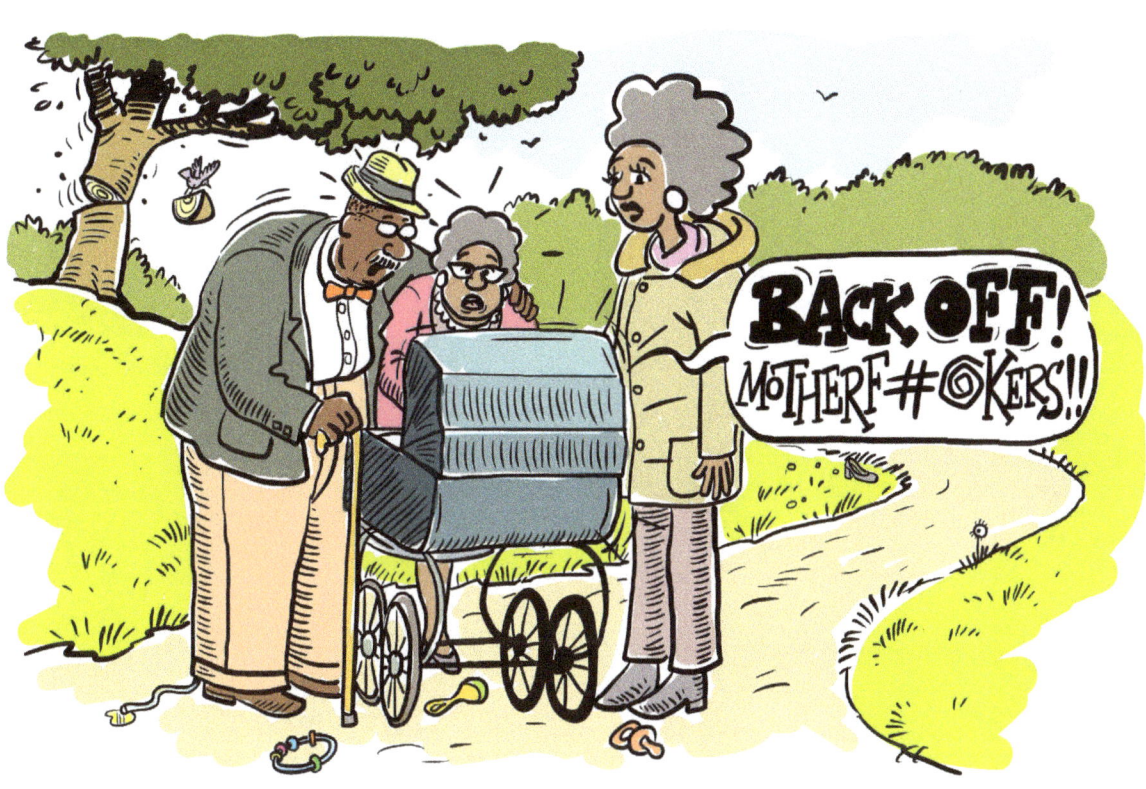

www.ingramcontent.com/pod-product-compliance
Lightning Source LLC
Chambersburg PA
CBHW061113070526
44583CB00027B/3279